IWO JIMA

P A C I F I C   O C E A N

KINAWA

TAIWAN
(FORMOSA)

Takao

Formosa Strait

LUZON

LEYTE

Manila

P H I L I P P I N E S

Hong Kong

Kiang

S O U T H   C H I N A   S E A

B O R N E O

Hanoi

FRENCH INDO-CHINA

Mekong

Saïgon

THAILAND
(SIAM)

Bangkok

Malay Peninsula

Singapore

Moulmein

rawaddy   Rangoon

S U M A T R A

A Y

F

GAL

Chennault and the Flying Tigers

Also by Anna Chennault

A THOUSAND SPRINGS:

The Biography of a Marriage

Anna Chennault

CHENNAULT
AND
THE FLYING TIGERS

Introduction by Thomas G. Corcoran

PAUL S. ERIKSSON, INC.

New York

To Governor James A. Noe of Louisiana, who, more than any other person, inspired me to write this book.

Preface

During the months that have passed since my book
A THOUSAND SPRINGS was first published, many
have asked where there exists a complete chronicle of
the life of my husband, Lieutenant General Claire
Lee Chennault, and the famous groups with which
he was associated—the American Volunteer Group,
the China Air Task Force, the Fourteenth Air Force,
and the Civil Air Transport—all his Flying Tigers.

Many books have been published dealing with one
or another aspect of General Chennault's life and
time; however, I do not know of any one volume
which contains, or can contain, the whole story of my
husband's long and eventful career. I have tried here
in one book, in one connected story, to tell for a new
generation what I consider the brightest highlights
of his brilliant career; the high points of a lifetime
devoted to service to his country and mankind.

I have drawn on my many years of close association
with my husband's work and with his contemporaries,
on innumerable conversations with the General and
"his men" and on the voluminous notes and diaries
he left, as well as my own. While I have a reporter's
memory for detail, I am not an aviation expert. But I
remember much; I have read widely; and I have here
tried faithfully to record what I have learned.

I have also made use of the writings of two perceptive men who knew and worked with the General. As an epilogue I have used in full Mr. Joseph Alsop's newspaper column, "The Old Hero," written just before his death; as a prologue I have used excerpts from a memoir written to me by Mr. Thomas Corcoran just after the General's death.

This is an account of one man's experiences in war and in peace—one who was sometimes almost cut off by the world because he did not choose to be a common man, because he preferred the challenge of life. He was a leader of men, but more than that, he was a leader of unusual men—The Flying Tigers. Together they proved that "faith can move mountains and lakes across ten thousand li."

I acknowledge my gratitude and indebtedness to many for their expert help and guidance in the preparation of this book: my brothers-in-law, William S., Joe Y., and Nelson Chennault—to Colonel Fred C. Milner, Brigadier General John R. Alison, General Tiger S. M. Wong, General Jerry J. L. Huang, Brigadier General Merian C. Cooper, Colonel P. Y. Shu, General Pai Chung Tsi, Robert C. Prescott, Colonel Wilfred Smith, Eloise Whitwer, Doreen Reynolds, Thomas G. Trumble, Hugh Grundy, George Doole, and to my sister, Cynthia Lee. I am grateful to them for many of the individual facts, anecdotes, and memories that form my image of the courageous, intrepid and inspired Claire Lee Chennault.

Anna Chennault

Washington, D. C.

Contents

List of Illustrations

Introduction

Was Chennault World War II's Lawrence of Arabia? Yes—but he was more than that.

The mass and velocity of Chennault's story are, of course, World War II while Lawrence's was World War I. The scene and the stakes here are the whole Far Eastern continent, instead of the Arabian desert. The logistics are the airplane, instead of the camel. And, although Chennault took the men of his former Chinese Air Force and built them into the Composite Wing of the Fourteenth Air Force, he actually immediately commanded a far larger number of Americans than Chinese.

The similarities between these highly individual—*individualistic*—men are, however, striking.

Each was a foreign military irregular who, for the benefit of his own country's professed political aims, took a leading part in the struggle for freedom of an ancient civilization alien to his native background. Each in his own heart and in the heart of a strange people became identified with the aspirations of that people who became tired of believing for too long too many so-called promises.

Each fought as passionately for a flaming personal cause as any Hospitaller in the Holy Land or the Grand Master in the gate at Malta. Did the rules of promotion and pay get in the way? Unimportant. Only *command* was important. Their creative imagination had to invent on the spot answers to the irregularly shaped realities for which there were no precedents. As the price for this inventiveness both Chennault and Lawrence were finally "relieved" of command by an institutionalized organization—military and political—whose very value to its so-

ciety was its training in the established ways which the
"lessons of the past" taught—and which in these guerrilla
situations these men faced didn't apply. But in neither
case did the man of imagination, of genius, "go" until he
had irrevocably changed the long course of history.

Each spectacularly fought imaginative "open" and,
most importantly, guerrilla wars—Lawrence Bedouins on
camels striking from the desert, Chennault fighter planes
hopping hit-and-run from one abandoned airfield to another. The determining factor in each case was what that
successful Chinese Communist, Mao Tse Tung, had said
about guerrilla warfare, "the guerrilla are the fish, the
people are the sea." With the Arabs Lawrence understood this intellectually. With the Chinese Chennault,
possibly alone among Americans, understood this from
experience because he had been for two years prior to
the Flying Tigers "one of us" among the Chinese and
knew their instinctive political and fighting patterns.

I sense there was another difference, a psychological
one. Lawrence was an emotional and intellectual solitary;
Chennault a gregarious sentimentalist. Chennault's heart
was warm and men homed to it.

So long as he had to kill 10 to 1, Chennault, like
Lawrence, (or his own hero, Stonewall Jackson) could be
coldly, sterilely professional. "Kill the bravest. The object
is to kill the enemy and do it as quickly as you can."
Above all he was professionally competent: he knew his
business, plane and gun, life and death.

But when he didn't have to be professional he had the
essential leadership gift of human warmth toward every
kind of man "on my side." Not only the Chinese warmed
back. Hard-boiled American "mercenaries" became romantic about him in China knowing that the boss who
played baseball with them had no illusions he was a god.

He enjoyed the solitude of the hunter and the fisherman but he was not a solitary. He had too much simple
faith in men and God to retire to brood over the ultimate evil of life; in "the aristocracy of those who care"

he was forever busy doing something about the evil. While Lawrence won and lost once before he was forty years old, and was philosopher enough not to go back to Arabia, Chennault won and lost at fifty in China and still came back to found CAT and a new way to use the spirit of the Flying Tigers. He is an inspiration, therefore, to both the young and to every man, forty or fifty and older.

Chennault, like Lawrence, was always in political trouble with his immediate, not his ultimate, superiors. In neither the China-Burma-India theatre of World War II nor in the Middle Eastern theatre of World War I could there be anything but political trouble. "Forgotten" China-Burma-India was a step-child theatre always deferred to the European main show. Its plans and supplies were always subject to change without notice as European fortunes changed. It had a complicated joint high command under the British, but Russia, France and Britain, too, all of whom had lost place or face in China and Asia, were constantly, understandably, plotting "in good faith" their post-war restoration or at least trying their best to see to it that the U. S. would not replace them. Even among Americans few besides Roosevelt and Chennault thought of the future of China for the sake of itself; for most, China was only a factor in the immediate defeat of Japan.

There is no way to know exactly what happens in a great war or why or who is "right." One thing is certain: no one gets what he wants or plans; deep currents of balancing forces repolarize old friends as new enemies, old enemies as new friends. The C-B-I theatre in particular fitted perfectly Justice Holmes' amused description of the Universe—"a jumping spontaneity taking irrational pleasure in moments of apparent rational sequence." And the great stone faces of the organization of mass war assume the interchangeability and replacement of parts and cannot afford the fighter-pilot independent originality of a successful genius like Chennault.

However, for the Chinese leaders who held together the resistance of their dogged peasants, Kunming and the Salween were salvation not from the hand of the foreign soldier, whose "help" for a hundred years they had learned to fear, but from a personal friend who, before America came into the war, had risked his own life for them. To him personally and to his airmen the Chinese thereafter gave the unstinting, unsuspicious cooperation they would give no other "foreigner."

As for Roosevelt, Chennault's exploits were a justification of an early faith and, like Clemenceau and Churchill, he felt that "war is much too important to be left to generals." Always he backed his faith in Chennault to the hilt and kept in constant personal communication with him. Chennault, fighting off accusations of "insubordination" to his intermediate military superiors, was insubordinately obeying his Commander in Chief. The risk and the price of this was of course that when Roosevelt failed Chennault would officially die too.

But, despite military and diplomatic politics, before Roosevelt would go and Chennault with him, there would pour into the beachhead of Chennault's little "mercenary" American Volunteer Group (the A.V.G.), first the official U. S. China Air Task Force, later the official U. S. Fourteenth Air Force, now Major General Chennault, USAF, commanding. Into that CATF and the 14th and the B-29 10th Air Force which the 14th protected, the magnetism of its record and its commander would pull every adventurous airman who could contrive his way into China.

The 14th was the smallest official U. S. Air Force. Without even minimal living conditions it operated from a home base nearly 7,000 feet high in a strange land with a strange language. Its supply lines were logistically impossible; they began with an air lift over the Himalayas; they ended with gasoline drums rolled miles by coolies into the forward bases. There was never enough gasoline or ammunition nor adequate ground protection for its bases which were surrounded by Japanese armies. But before Chennault left, by the genius bred of necessity, the 14th had demonstrated as no other air force before or since, the uttermost limits of what airmen and air power, man for man and plane for plane, can do. It completely destroyed the Japanese Air Force in South Asia. It broke the Japanese land armies who had hoped to dig in in China. To help MacArthur and Kenney conquer the Pacific it bombed Tokyo and Formosa, 3,500 miles from its nearest ship supply at Calcutta.

Chennault and his Tigers were this manner of men.

I like to remember three meetings—the first time I met him (Note from Mrs. Chennault: "I have included this in my book"—so I won't tell it here), the last time I hunted with him, the last walk on Bunker Hill.

Deer season, 1956, I went hunting with him down in his camp in Tensas, Louisiana. I slept in the room with him and for the first time realized from the way he breathed how real was his physical danger.

We got up early in the morning to take positions where the dogs could drive by us. Max Chennault and Ben Chase were to organize the dogs.

The General and I started out early to take positions after a breakfast of those canned oysters he liked so much. As we walked through the woods I noticed that he had to stop every hundred feet "to be quiet."

When we finally got to positions, he characteristically gave me the best one at a V-bend of a wood road—a long clean line of sight. His position was probably a hundred yards to the right of me.

It was a soft dreamy morning with mist coming up from the river. I heard but didn't see the dogs coming up on my right making a racket. I thought they went through the General's position—but there were no shots. I was just as pleased nothing came my way. I would not have wanted to fail a shot and lose face but I had long ago passed the point where I felt that I had to kill deer.

About half an hour after the dogs went by the General came up the road toward me. "I didn't hear you fire. See anything?"

"No. I didn't hear you either."

"I'm afraid they went by us," he said. "Let's go back. It's too late now."

We walked down the road together to the camp passing a "rice paddy" in which he had planted millet and rice for birds and ducks (fed with a pump from the river). He stopped to admire the birds—excited over this "conservation project"—and the hundreds of birds it brought. For the first time I saw literally in flocks what I called "cardinals"—he called them "redbirds."

As we left the "paddy" he said, "Were you disappointed you didn't get a shot?"

I said, "To your ears alone, no. I've passed the point where I like to kill deer."

"Then since you've said that I'll tell you something, ears alone for you. Except that I was afraid you'd be disappointed, I wasn't disappointed either. I've also reached the point where I would rather see them alive and beautiful and jumping and waving their white tails than just a hunk of meat. I'm past that point, too. Well, as long as we didn't get a deer, let's go down and get some fish. I don't feel the same way about fish."

We went down to the river, tied up on the bank in the "best place"—got talking about China, politics, everything under the sun—looked up at the end of three hours and neither of us had even begun to catch a fish. We went back to the camp for lunch and had some more canned oysters with Ben Chase. Some hunters; some fishermen!

The day the General insisted Lahey Clinic tell him the truth, he learned that his cancer was incurable as far as they were concerned and that he had only six months to live. That day he and I were about to take a ride to see the "Yankee Revolutionary War." The General had never "seen" Revolutionary Boston before. The doctors told me, before the General and I got in the car, that the General had had this talk with them and that he had received the bad news. All day long I didn't mention the cancer to the General nor he the cancer to me.

We rode down in Dr. Sara Jordan's car to Bunker Hill. We climbed Bunker Hill. The General assessed the military situation at a glance and launched into contempt for a British general who with an easy way out of the situation by just cutting across Charleston Neck had lost troops in a frontal assault. "A General who did that should be court-martialed and shot. That was as stupid as sending out bombers without fighter escort. The first job of a general is to keep losses down."

We visited the "Constitution" lying in Boston Harbor. We went below to the gun deck and looked over the main battery. I got a lesson on fire power and the N-square concentration of fire power and "So this is Boston Harbor —the Old North Church—and the British fleet. You could take out the whole place today with two good bombers."

We rode out to Lexington, paced off Lexington Green —and I got another lesson, this time on the significance of the situation in China when the countryside was for us as it here had been against the British.

Then we went to Concord and walked over "the bridge that arched the flood." This time the lesson was on "farm boys like me" who were realists enough to have a sense of private property and courage to fight to protect what they had instead of promoting a lot of ideologies.

We rode back still educating. As we came into the hospital the General said very casually: "I have been thinking it over and I think I'd better get back to Formosa right away. We have spent as much time as we can afford to spend here."

"Isn't the Formosa trip something that is rather long and tiring at this time? Don't you think we ought to stay with the doctors a little longer?"

"I think I'd rather get over to Formosa and get my
business done right away because the trip will be easier
on Anna and the children at this time of the year and
I'd like to be back after New Year. Let's plan to get out
of here and I'll get about my business in Formosa right
away. I think I'll have dinner alone in my room tonight:
I want to do some writing. This was a lovely day. Thank
you. I'll always remember it. Maybe you Damyankees had
something after all. I almost think I could learn to like
them. Good night."

This is "as I remember him."

Forget the intrigues of the inter-allied struggle for
"face" in the forgotten theatre of China-Burma-India.
Forget the illusions of the inter-allied struggle for power
in the post war period in China. Too much and too many
were involved in these disasters of the democratic process
ever to prove anyone was "right."

Remember only the courage, skill and devotion
"through the last ditch and beyond" of a commander
who, his peers say, did more with less than any American
commander of the war.

Remember only his Flying Tigers, farthest away from
home of any American fighting men, facing without supplies and "against fearful odds" the full brunt of the
Japanese war machine at its highest peak—and winning
when we most needed victory.

Remember Joe Alsop's "Old Hero," sixty, still fighting
with only his private air line "to buy the West time to
wake up"—the last plane out of crumbling Canton, the
last plane out of burning Seoul, the last plane *into* dying
Dien Bien Phu.

"Courage," someone has said, "is grace under pressure."

Excerpts from a memoir by
Thomas G. Corcoran

"Thus kings were people who worked a thousand times harder than the people, without benefit to themselves. This was hardly an enviable position. Therefore, there were those who worked for the benefit of the public and never wanted to be called kings . . ."

Huang Tsungshi
Ming Dynasty (1610-1695)

Part **1** Early Years

> "..........the twig is bent,
>   so grows the tree."

Chapter 1

"Now he has come back to us forever."

The speaker was Madame Chiang Kai-shek who was standing beside me; the time April, 1960, a year and some months after the death of Lt. General Claire Lee Chennault. The occasion was the unveiling of a life-size bronze bust of General Chennault in a place of great honor in Taipei, Taiwan, near the national capital building.

"We owe so much to Claire," said my sister Cynthia, who was a nurse for the Flying Tigers, and now Mrs. Richard Lee.

And I was reminded of what the commander of the Japanese forces in Central China, Lieutenant General Takahashi, said after World War II. He said that General Chennault's 14th Air Force constituted between sixty and seventy-five percent of the effective opposition Japan faced in China. Without the 14th Air Force, he believed the Japanese forces could have pushed anywhere they wished in China.

"My husband was happy to serve China for two reasons," I said. "He loved China and the Chinese people. But beyond that, he was convinced, even before he arrived in China in 1937, that by helping China fight the Japanese he was helping his own country."

My mind travelled backward in time to that day of farewell in 1945 in China's wartime capital, Chungking. World War II was not quite over but

4

General Chennault, his mission accomplished, was leaving China. His "Flying Tigers" had annihilated the Japanese air force. Japan's ground forces were in disorganized retreat. She had lost the war in China.

The greatest crowd in Chungking's history turned out to bid Chennault farewell. The Generalissimo had sent his car for him but the people, perhaps two million of them, choked the streets from wall to wall. They waved from windows, and from balconies, and from roof-tops. The chauffeur couldn't drive through the happy throngs in the streets. He turned off his engine and the people pushed the car along with their hands. It was a tremendous demonstration of affection. General Chennault was undoubtedly the most famous and best-loved foreigner the people of China have ever known.

It was a day of triumph and sadness for my husband—triumph over the Japanese invaders and incredible military odds; sadness because for reasons hard to understand, and harder to endure, he was leaving China not because of the invaders, whom he had defeated, but because of his fellow-Americans who had held back his supplies and sought to discredit him.

But General Chennault's record speaks for itself. During three years of handicapped operations, outnumbered twenty to one in the air and threatened by victorious enemy ground forces, Chennault and his Flying Tigers became a living legend.

His men were greeted everywhere with smiles, upraised thumbs, and the cry of *"Ding Hao"* (Top Good!). In the air their ratio of victory was ten Japanese planes shot down for every single American plane lost.

Madame Chiang's soft voice brought me back to Taipei, 1960. "You know, Anna," she said, "I am glad that he lived long enough for his country to honor him in his lifetime. It would have been tragic if he had died feeling unappreciated. I'm glad he knew that your President had honored him with a third star, making him Lieutenant General Chennault."

There had been other honors, too, the final great homage paid by his country and his contemporaries as he was laid to rest in Arlington National Cemetery. Hundreds of notables, and countless others—more than five thousand in all—attended, and the greatest of his country's military and political leaders served as honorary pall bearers. The last time I had seen Madame Chiang was on that sad day in July of 1958.

This was Claire Lee Chennault, the soldier who twice in his long career had been dropped from his country's military rosters—both times officially asking for retirement for "reasons of health"—but actually being forced out both times for being much, much too tactlessly, annoyingly, and everlastingly *right* about many things.

This was the man for whom in 1945 Chungking was gaily bedecked, the man who stood on a platform all morning and far into the afternoon shaking the hands of Chinese well-wishers who were grateful to "Chennote Chiang Chun," as they called him, for saving their country from the Japanese invaders.

And this was the same Claire Lee Chennault whose application for flight training, when the United States declared war on Germany in 1917, was rejected with the comment: "Applicant does not possess necessary qualifications for a successful aviator."

Chapter 2

Claire Chennault's urge to fly was born on a hot summer day in 1903 in eastern Louisiana where the still, moist air over the Tensas River lay heavy with cloying fragrance. The only sound was the lazy droning of omnipresent insects; the only motion the darting dragonflies on the water's surface—and the alert dark eyes of the boy, Claire, as he lounged on the river's bank.

Those eyes, deep-set and piercing, and almost as dark as the heavy shock of black hair, were fixed on a patch of sky visible through a break in the branches overhead. High in the blue air a hawk wheeled with lazy, effortless ease and the boy was lost in admiration.

"How tremendous!" he thought and then, like Icarus and countless others before and since: "How I'd love to fly like that!"

The hawk swooped suddenly, toward an unseen prey, and the boy's eyes followed the swift dramatic dive until tree branches along the river bank hid the final scene. His gaze shifted to the dragonflies sweeping the surface of the water for smaller insects, their silvery wings flashing in the leaf-filtered sunshine. How quick and sure, he thought, were their darting movements. They, like the hawk high above, were skillful fliers.

He thought, now, briefly, of other flyers—the wild

ducks, the wild turkeys. He had studied their flight
habits carefully, for he liked to hunt them and he
could not afford to waste a shot. To miss what he
aimed at was a serious error and a costly one. Ammunition was expensive to a boy whose only means of
acquiring it was through long hours of farm work at
low wages. Claire had to make every shot count, and
early in life became an expert shot with rifle and shot-
gun, the best marksman in the district.

His father, to his death at the age of eighty-two,
talked proudly of Claire's prowess with a rifle, believing firmly that this skill helped him to defeat the
Japanese airmen.

In a sense it did. "A wasted bullet might mean a
wasted life—yours!" he pounded home to his students, the trainees of the American Volunteer Group,
and the 14th Air Force, years later, when he was their
commanding officer in Burma and China.

"Conserve your ammunition," he would tell them,
"don't just keep firing your gun hoping one of your
bullets will hit the enemy. One well aimed bullet will
do the job, *but it must be well aimed!*"

The mind of the boy dreaming by the Tensas river
returned now, for the thousandth time, to a story he
had read in a newspaper a few weeks ago; a story so
fascinating, so exciting that his heart leaped every
time he thought of it. Two brothers named Wright
had built a flying machine and were ready to try it
out.

"Wings!" "Flight!" These were magic words to this

lean, sun-browned boy, Claire Lee Chennault, in this historic year, 1903. Up to now, the rugged, outdoor life of the wild Louisiana woods and daring adventures—his own and those of the heroes in the books he loved to read—were the stuff of which Claire Chennault's dreams were made. Now, the heady thought of flying high above the earth, in a flying machine had become the greatest of his dreams. Nothing, he was sure, could surpass the thrill of flying. And, in all of Claire Chennault's later life, nothing ever did.

In the weeks following the newspaper story of the Wright brothers and their flying machine, Claire Chennault's future career was shaped as surely as though his father, Stonewall Jackson Chennault, had planned and blueprinted it. His father, as a matter of fact, was skeptical of man's ability to fly.

"If the Lord had intended men to fly, He would have put wings on their shoulders!" he had observed, in response to Claire's enthusiastic reaction to the story of the Wright brothers' flying machine.

But Stonewall Jackson Chennault's words failed to dampen Claire's enthusiasm in the slightest.

Late in December of the same year the newspapers carried banner headlines. The Wright brothers had kept a flying machine aloft at Kitty Hawk, North Carolina, for fifty-nine seconds at a speed of thirty miles an hour. It was Claire Chennault's greatest thrill since he'd shot his first wild turkey with his first rifle. Now the sky was man's new frontier and he would be part of it for he was only ten years old. There would be no stopping him.

Given the heritage of this strong-jawed boy, plus his love of adventurous physical accomplishment, and his intense admiration for real and legendary heroes, there was little wonder that his pioneer spirit should focus on man's flight as the most exciting dream of his life.

It was, moreover, not very strange that his love of flying should later be successfully combined with a military career. For soldiering and the pioneer spirit ran strongly through his lineage.

In 1778 when the Marquis de Lafayette issued his call for French volunteers to aid the American colonists in their struggle for independence from England, three Chennault brothers had responded. They were Huguenots, residing in Alsace-Lorraine.

One of these, Steven Chennault, who after the Revolutionary War became a Virginia tobacco planter, was the ancestor of Claire Lee Chennault. The same courageous, pioneering urge to explore new frontiers was transmitted to Steven's sons, one of whom, John Nelson, roamed gun in hand through virgin forests until he came to an unsettled frontier region called Tennessee. Later, John Nelson pushed further on, into the Carolinas and, somewhere in his travels, he came to rest long enough to woo and wed Hanna Houston, a first cousin of Sam Houston.

Sam Houston! No other American hero, unless it were Daniel Boone, had a greater direct and indirect effect on the character and career of Claire Chennault. For not only did the Houston blood run in Claire's veins, but he read with avid interest every account he could find of the adventurous life of the fabulous Tennessean who had scandalized his friends and neighbors by going to live with the Indians; who had won the battle of San Jacinto and captured Santa Anna when his little army was outnumbered ten to one; who had loved the United States of America so much that he resigned as Governor of Texas rather than see Texas secede from the Union.

Robert E. Lee! Other great Southern blood flowed in the Chennault veins—the blood of the family of General Robert E. Lee.

Steven was the name given to the son of Hanna Houston and John Nelson Chennault after John Nelson's father. As the boy grew up, the restless Chennault spirit set him wandering south and west in search of wilder country. Eventually he paused in the Louisiana delta country where he married Frances Thomson, who bore him a son, John Stonewall Jackson Chennault.

True to the family tradition, John Stonewall Jackson Chennault grew up as wild as some of the wooded delta country through which he loved to hunt and fish. His exuberance delayed, for a time, the consent of Jessie Lee to marry him. Jessie, a cousin of Robert E. Lee, the Confederate military genius, thought John a little wild for a prospective husband. But here another Chennault quality, dogged persistence, came to John's aid and finally they were married.

Jessie herself was a persistent young woman, taking after her father, Dr. William Wallace Lee, a surgeon in the Army of Virginia. When General Robert E. Lee regretfully and resignedly surrendered to Grant at Appomattox Court House, Dr. Lee hid out until dark and kept going. He never did surrender.

The son of Jessie Lee and John Stonewall Jackson Chennault, Claire Lee Chennault, was born in Commerce, Texas, in 1893.*

And here in the early character and exploits, and the later successes we see, I think, the effect of a blood line that included the genes of the Houstons and the Lees; a heritage that included a father named after Stonewall Jackson; ancestors who fought with Lafayette for Washington. And to all of this was added the martial heritage of the proud American South.

Once, in Kunming, I asked a group of the General's boys a question that occurred to me simply because every one of them in the room at the time was, like the General himself, from the South.

Lounging around the living room of the General's bungalow were several of the great flying aces of World War II. There were Bob Scott, Johnny Alison, Tex Hill, and Ed Rector.

"Tell me," I asked, "why so many Southern boys

---

* Chennault had three brothers: William S. Chennault, Sweetwater, Texas; Nelson Chennault, San Antonio, Texas; Joe Y. Chennault, Washington, D. C.

choose military careers—and why so many of them—
like yourselves—are so good at it."

They were personally modest and I had embar-
rassed them, but about their Southern background
and what it meant they were articulate. There were
several reasons, they said, why a Southern boy might
be attracted toward a career in the armed forces. To
begin with, the South in their day was mainly agricul-
tural. It lacked the economic power and commercial
opportunities which the North could offer to its restless young men.

The South in the early 1900's had no background
of sectional wealth, or economic power, or big industrial plants for a boy to be proud of. There were the
tobacco and cotton and watermelon fields, but if a
boy chose not to be a planter, what else was open to
him, should he be restless, ambitious, and energetic?

For Southern Americans of Claire Chennault's generation, and even those of the generation of Alison
and Rector, there just wasn't as much scope or opportunity in the South as in the richer, more industrial-
ized, more commercial North.

But the post-reconstruction generation of South-
erners to which Claire Chennault's father had be-
longed was a proud heritage. John Stonewall Jackson
Chennault had Stonewall Jackson to be proud of, and
Pickett's men who charged at Gettysburg when
Yankees would undoubtedly have been more prudent.
True, the Confederacy had lost the war, but every
boy of military age had served, and the war, as they

saw it, had been lost to the North's factories, money, and man power. The Southern forces, lacking the North's resources, had fought heroically under brilliant leaders against tremendous odds.

Southern boys, not having wealth to boast of, were fiercely proud of the fighting qualities of their ancestors and of their war heroes, Lee and Jackson and the others.

It was with such an inheritance, and against such a background that Claire Lee Chennault grew toward manhood—deeply conscious of his background, fiercely conscious of the American heroes; he himself became a youthful reincarnation of Daniel Boone, Sam Houston, Huckleberry Finn—and Orville Wright.

Often he tried the patience of his stepmother—his own mother died when he was very young—by disappearing into the Louisiana oak woods and moss-draped cypress swamps for days at a time, hunting and fishing, exploring what was over the next rise or across the next stream. He lived on berries and the game he shot, and slept on beds he made of moss and boughs under lean-tos he had built.

Very early in life Claire Chennault realized that nothing came on a silver platter, that if he wanted something he either earned the money to buy it or made it with his own hands. He did odd jobs for his neighbors, clearing fields of stones, weeding gardens or chopping wood. Most of the money went into guns and ammunition.

Despite his wanderings through the woods and swamps of the Louisiana bayou country that sometimes lasted for days at a time, he did not neglect his education. In grade school, he delighted his teacher with his knowledge of history, particularly the history of great fighting men and the battles of Marathon, Thermopylae, and Cannae. He poured over them, imagining what he would have done had he been the generals in those battles.

Because his ancestors had served George Washington, he studied the life of the first President. Learning that Washington had read and admired Plutarch, Claire Chennault read—and admired and was influenced by—Plutarch.

As might have been expected of a wilderness hunter, he was a topnotch athlete in three sports, baseball, basketball, and football, a boy of fast mental reaction and physical coordination. These physical and mental qualities stood him in good stead from the time his mother died and he had to take care of himself, throughout his young manhood and later life. His coordination and perfect timing saw him through many aerial dogfights against skillful and dedicated Japanese pilots in the skies over China. It has been stated unofficially, but by those who are in a position to know, that Chennault was the greatest of all World War II aces, having personally destroyed at least 40 Japanese planes in aerial combat during his early days in China before the United States entered the conflict.

In his teens, Chennault promised to be a lean and rugged man. His keen eyes looked out on the world from a face heavily bronzed by countless hours spent in the open. In their depths was a tolerance and kindness that in later years was to earn the love and loyalty of American fighting men.

The greater part of his early years, spent mostly alone in the wild country, taught him self-reliance and gave him self confidence. They made him reflective and inventive. He always refused to recognize the "impossible." In the wild life of the Louisiana woods which he loved and in which he felt so at home, there was no percentage in recognizing the "impossible." You succeeded in doing what was necessary for survival or you didn't come out of the woods alive.

This same willingness—even eagerness—to take on "impossible" odds and tasks is seen time and again throughout his career. This was the same boy who, on a dare, stepped into a brackish stream and turned over a six-foot alligator; who years later put a "Jenny" bi-plane through acrobatics others said the plane couldn't possibly perform; who still later hurled his tiny group of American volunteers against Japan's air force and achieved total victory against twenty-to-one odds.

He could outrun and outwit every boy in the neighborhood and once led some of his playmates a twenty-mile chase cross-country, over streams and through deepest woods, and swampy stretches veteran woodsmen considered impassable.

From his grandfather's old Negro servant he had

learned rough and tumble fighting tricks involving the use of head and feet as well as fists, a necessary education in those days if a plantation boy wished to survive and hold his head up.

The early days in the woods helped to mold the qualities of mind and character that were to place him among the most expert military minds of the century, especially in the open, guerrilla-type war he later found in China.

Inevitably, the time arrived when the elders in the Chennault household decreed that something had to be done about changing Claire from a roving hunter and fisherman to something resembling a finished scholar. Uncle Nelson Chennault, a teacher, conferred with Claire's father, who agreed that his son could not make a career out of roaming the bayous.

"What do you want to be—to study for?" his father asked him.

"I'd like to fly an airplane," Claire answered promptly.

His father and his uncle glanced at each other, then back at the boy.

"Flying is new—experimental," his uncle pointed out. "What sort of career appeals to you—something real you can study for now?"

The boy thought a moment. "I guess I'd like to go to West Point or Annapolis."

The two men nodded approvingly, but the boy's dark eyes were looking out the window toward the sky beyond the trees.

But I'd still rather fly! he thought to himself.

Chapter 3

Claire submitted applications to both West Point and the Naval Academy, and in 1909 he went to Annapolis to take entrance examinations. After two days spent in frowning concentration over the examinations, he learned that midshipmen were confined to the Academy for their first two years. A thoughtful look at the grim gray walls of the Academy did the rest. He couldn't stand the thought of two years behind them. He turned in a blank final exam paper and returned to his beloved Louisiana, where it was decided that he should attend Louisiana State University.

Despite his athletic achievements at Baton Rouge, young Chennault found life as a freshman hard to bear. The city boys were clannish, inclined to look down their noses at students from the hinterland. Never one to play second fiddle, he decided after being ignored and barred from a college fraternity to form one of his own. The first members were his brother, Bill, and another youngster from Gilbert, Louisiana. The rules were simple. You pledged friendship and help to one another. Appropriately, the fraternity's symbol was an alligator.

From the moment he applied for training in the University Cadet Corps, he got his first tastes of military regulations and discipline. On the morning following his acceptance he was hazed by his military superiors and sheared of his thick black hair.

His impatience with cadet "spit and polish" foreshadowed the kind of difficulties he would face throughout his military career when he was pressured to follow and to enforce what seemed to him—as to Sam Houston—senseless rules and regulations which might have disciplinary value in military academies but had little value in combat situations. Years later in China, when his command was short of aviation gasoline and other vital supplies; when he was using black, re-drained engine oil in his P-40's yet all the while managing to chalk up the finest record of aerial victory in air annals, he was accused by a theater headquarters officer of not insisting that his men keep their jackets buttoned and their buttons polished.

Choking back the angry words he would have liked to utter, he led the desk officer to a newly prepared wall chart showing the impressive 10-to-1 ratio of victory.

"I don't think spit and polish is going to help these boys improve their record," he drawled. "And I don't think it matters to those dead Japs whether my men had their jackets buttoned!"

But although he always scorned empty superficialities, he had great respect for the deeper, more meaningful attributes of a good soldier—dependability, courage, firmness, willingness to give one's best unstintingly.

The Seniors at Louisiana State kept at him. One

night the cadet captain ordered him to stand guard under a window of the old barracks and instructed him to let no one pass. He was to stay until relieved. Water began pouring onto his head from a window directly above him. There was loud snickering. He did not move, and a fierce grin stretched his lips thin. The fun finally wore off and the Seniors left the barracks and made their way to their sleeping quarters. They had to pass the "guard" they'd posted. Claire Chennault, laughing deep within, reminded them that he had been given orders that no one was to pass his post. They argued, tried to get by forcibly only to get a rifle barrel slammed across their chests. "I'm stayin' on guard, as ordered, until my relief comes. A good soldier always obeys orders," he said in his rich Southern drawl.

The ring-leader at last decided to send for a guard to relieve the drenched but determined Freshman Cadet.

At the end of the third school year, he returned home to Gilbert, deciding to take a long vacation wandering through his old haunts with gun and fishing rod before hunting for a summer job that would pay him enough to complete his college education.

During the summer, his uncle, Nelson Chennault, reminded Claire that he possessed the knack of showing others how to do things and suggested that he spend his last college year at State Normal School taking a teaching course. Nelson offered to advance him the tuition fees and Claire gratefully accepted.

This was the start of a lifelong teaching career.

Most officers spend a considerable part of their careers teaching others, or being taught. Claire Chennault was a teacher all his life. The articles he later wrote for the service magazines, setting forth his theories of air tactics were part of his continuous efforts to impart knowledge.

But his greatest and most successful teaching career began in the Burma jungles and continued on the plains of China's Yunnan province as he taught the Flying Tigers how to defeat the Japanese in the air and live to tell of it.

In this airman's school, the reward for scholastic brilliance was fame and honor; the penalty of lessons poorly learned was death at the hands of skillful, well-drilled, fanatically dedicated Japanese pilots. The incredible success of the Flying Tigers was a triumph of patient, careful teaching. But that all came many years later.

At Louisiana State Normal College (now Northwestern State College at Natchitoches) he discovered his Uncle Nelson's opinion of his talents had not been the biased talk of a relative. He found teaching deeply satisfying and graduated with flying colors, considered by the faculty to be one of the most capable scholars ever to attend the school. Teaching jobs, however, were few and far between. A batch of letters of application produced nothing but disappointments. Resignedly, he went to work doing odd jobs at odd hours on the surrounding plantations, wondering if the life of a Kit Carson or Jim Bridger was destined to be his lot. Then, one day his chance came.

Over in the little parish of Franklin, Louisiana, the town fathers were facing a serious problem. Schoolteachers were finding their pupils too unruly to handle. The tough backwoods boys had chased one teacher after another to healthier climates. The parish authorities were on the verge of closing the school when a visitor from Gilbert asked the head of the school board if he had ever heard of Claire Chennault. This young teacher, the visitor stated, could lick his weight in wildcats and feared neither man nor beast.

The parish fathers somewhat doubtfully agreed to give young Chennault a chance to prove his mettle both as a disciplinarian and as an instructor.

In due time Claire presented himself at the one-room clapboard schoolhouse in Athens, Louisiana. Reports, he immediately decided, eyeing the class, had not been exaggerated. There was downright deviltry and scorn in a dozen pairs of eyes, and he stood and traded glance for glance before he got down to opening a book.

For the first few minutes of his first day everything seemed well under control, and then, when he turned his back for a moment, a blackboard eraser skimmed close to his ear and bounded off the wall. Slowly, he turned and inquired, "All right, who threw that?" The students grinned and for several charged moments no one spoke.

"Who threw it?" Chennault asked once more. Finally a husky farm boy said defiantly, "I did. You maybe aim to do somethin' about it?"

Claire Chennault walked slowly to the student's desk. "Stand up!" he snapped, and when the big youth obeyed he thrust his strong jaw close to the trouble-maker's nose. "Yes, we're going to do something about it. Let's go outside!" His eyes raked the others. "Class dismissed. You can all watch if you wish."

"Sure," the culprit said scornfully, "somebody's got to tote him off when I'm finished with him."

Neither teacher nor pupil wasted any time, and it was the farm boy who got the surprise of his life. He soon discovered that although he outweighed this im-placable, gimlet-eyed teacher by fifty pounds, he had more than met his match. This teacher knew as many fighting tricks, clean and otherwise, as he did—and a few more. The boy fought hard, for his pride was at stake. But he was up against a man of lightning-fast reflexes; a man with muscles like steel springs; a man of reckless courage and incredible determination. Soon, badly bruised, blood streaming from his nose, an eye closing fast, the farm boy called it quits.

It was not the first time—and far from the last—that Claire Chennault faced heavy odds unafraid, and won. Years later the Japanese air force, much larger than Chennault's, learned how well he could fight against outsized enemies.

That first encounter with his charges was not Claire Chennault's last. Before reasonable order came to the little schoolhouse of Franklin parish the lean young teacher held bare-knuckle decisions over half the class. Finally, he channeled the boys' turbulent ener-gies into athletics, and from that time on the school began to capture most of the championships in three sports in that part of the state. This was one of Claire Chennault's first proving grounds. Here he received his basic training in the complex art of handling and understanding men.

He remained at the little Athens, Louisiana, school for almost four years, fully content with his lot. He loved the teaching profession, and school closed early in the spring so the students could help with the planting. Classes did not resume until after the fall harvest. This gave him plenty of time between terms to hunt and fish, read up on military tactics, and keep himself informed in the advancing field of aviation. Finally, however, he left Franklin parish and moved from job to job until one came along that fitted in with his growing purpose: to fly an airplane.

At Akron, Ohio, where kite balloons were being manufactured, he became an inspector of these new inflated lighter-than-air gas bags that were to be labeled "sausages" during World War I. They were designed for observation over enemy lines, and were fitted with an extra airbag at the rear to keep them in a stable position.

In Europe the rumbles of impending conflict were growing more ominous, and in 1917 the United States was brought into the war that had driven both England and France nearly to their knees. Claire Chennault answered the first call for American volunteers and on November 27, 1917, emerged from Officers' Training School, Fort Benjamin Harrison, Indiana, as a "ninety-day wonder." He was a first lieutenant in the infantry, but as far as his plans were concerned it was simply the first step toward an airplane cockpit.

Because of his balloon experience in Akron, it seemed natural to volunteer for the kite-balloon section of the Signal Corps. He was accepted. At last he was on his way, he thought elatedly, to getting off the ground. But after a few months had passed he grew restless.

A captive balloon tied to a truck isn't going anywhere unless it breaks away, and then it is useless. Overseas the British and French were flying heavier-than-air planes armed with machine guns against the German Fokkers, Taubes, and Gothas. This was the kind of flying of which Lieutenant Claire Chennault continued to dream and to strive toward.

After several weeks of duty at Fort Travis, Texas, he heard that Army engineers were clearing a cotton plantation not far away. On a hunch, he investigated and learned that the aviation section of the Signal Corps was building an airfield where pilots would be trained to fly the Curtiss JN-4, the "Jenny." A fellow officer, eyeing one of the fragile planes, scornfully remarked that it was a flying coffin, a "mish-mash of spruce sticks, doped fabric, and piano wire, all held together with glue."

Claire Chennault gave his fellow officer the full force of his impatience. The Jenny could fly, and fly well, he was convinced. He set out to prove it.

Chapter 4

Like the "impassable" swamps area of Louisiana Claire Chennault had successfully explored, the Jenny was a new challenge to be met, a new adversary to be conquered.

To understand why in the period of his sorest trials he never gave up no matter how heavy the odds or trying the vicissitudes, one needs only to look at the difficulties this World War II ace-to-be overcame in order even to be allowed to risk his neck for his country!

At every opportunity he was at newly completed Kelly Field. The racket from the noisy biplanes was as soothing to his ears as the nocturnal serenade of the night creatures in his native canebrakes. The harsh roar of their propellers and the strange rattling, singing sound they made in flight fascinated him. He envied the men who flew them.

The Army, with reports coming in from France on the exploits of the Lafayette Escadrille, the British R.F.C., and the German ace, Richthofen, called for volunteers to start pilot training. Chennault immediately applied to the selection board, was questioned at length, and given a careful physical checkup. He went back to his humdrum work on the ground and waited. A few days later he received a rejection notice stating that he did not possess the "necessary qualifications."

Swallowing the setback as best he could, Chennault remained at Kelly for a year, putting green aviation cadets through infantry drill. Three more times he applied for flight training and was three times refused, and one day he decided he would not go "by the book" any longer. Carefully and deliberately, he cultivated and nurtured an acquaintance with several genial instructors at Kelly, among them a seasoned flier named Charley Leonard who agreed to familiarize him with the fundamentals of flying the temperamental Jenny.

Proving himself an apt pupil, he induced the instructor to solo him unofficially. "Go ahead and kill yourself, Lieutenant," Leonard roared, "but please do us a favor and make the splash off the limits of the field!"

Chennault, a slow grin wreathing his tanned face, took the Jenny off the ground and put it through maneuvers that made the instructor wince. Momentarily he expected to see a wing fly off and the Jenny start spinning toward the hard-packed Texas earth. His "pupil" kept circling until Leonard was afraid Chennault would have to make a dead-stick landing, and he frantically waved him down. The Jenny glided in and landed, and Chennault stepped out of the cockpit and patted the Jenny's fuselage. The grin he gave Leonard was slowly returned. "This boy," the old instructor thought, with pride in his own judgment, "can really fly!"

Claire Chennault's next step was to scheme his way

into an assignment at a nearby staging area where he was in charge of gassing and checking training planes. He loved working on airplanes, but best of all he was now in a position to occasionally "borrow" a Jenny and get in some flying time.

"Once I flew off to Dallas," he confessed, long afterward, "and was A.W.O.L. for a week. They never missed me or the plane."

Orders whisked him away from the paradise on JN-4's to Fort Ellington, to Fort Bliss, and to Gernster Field in his native Louisiana. Somehow, as always, his confidence in himself seemed to irritate his superiors. In addition he had the unfortunate habit of being right much too often for the peace of mind of any supervisors. He seemed to be drawing assignments for everything but flying and he was beginning to chafe. With the advent of autumn, his hopes soared when orders came through naming him adjutant of the 46th Fighter Squadron at Mitchell Field. On arrival he was told the outfit would soon be sent overseas.

The 46th Fighter Squadron did actually start out for the port of embarkation, but halfway there the orders were rescinded. An armistice was in sight in Europe.

Back at Kelly Field, Chennault managed to pick up eighty more hours of "bootleg" flying before official instruction began. After clashing with an Army flight instructor as fiery-tempered as himself he found himself washed out of the Air Corps once more.

Somewhat humbled, but as determined as ever,

Chennault asked the Washout Board for one more chance. He had been wrong, he admitted; the instructor had been right. He knew he was a good pilot and wanted a last chance to prove it. After much deliberation, his request was granted, and a few weeks later he was putting the fragile, unpredictable Jenny through acrobatics—something even the oldest instructors shied at. In the spring of 1919, the rating "fighter pilot" was at last put on his record.

His honorable discharge from his reserve commission in the wartime Army came through a year later on April 9, 1920, and he returned to his cotton plantation to await action on his request for a regular commission in the newly organized Air Service of the regular Army. The summer months dragged by, and he divided his time between work on his acres, and his beloved hunting and fishing. The familiar surroundings of his boyhood worked away many of the frustrations that nagged him. He was footloose again, and fancy free. He had flown as high as the hawk!

His commission arrived on September 14, 1920, and the following summer he was accepted for the first fighter pilot course with the 94th Fighter Squadron, one that had spilled blood in France, and commanded by Frank "Monk" Hunter, World War I ace. It was the famous "hat in the ring" squadron which had included Eddie Rickenbacker, who in Claire Chennault's formative flying years was his inspiration and who, after World War II, became Chennault's staunch admirer.

In the summer of 1963, Capt. Eddie Rickenbacker,

a hero in his own right and knowledgeable in matters of aerial warfare, told me during one of the "Tonight" television programs on which we appeared, with Arthur Godfrey as host: "In proportion to what General Chennault was given to work with, Chennault's was the outstanding individual American achievement of World War II."

For four months following the granting of his commission, Claire Chennault flew all over the Texas sky, emulating Western Front individual dogfight flying. He quickly became convinced such medieval jousting tactics would not work in another war. This was fun as a sport and it had been quite the thing in World War I, but it would be all wrong in another, more modern war, to his way of thinking. It lacked the advantages of team work, and it violated sound military precepts by dispersing, instead of concentrating, force and firepower.

The bemedalled veterans of the Squadron were somewhat patronizing in their treatment of the air freshmen, and their "new-fangled" ideas. A fellow student, Joe Cannon, was nearly killed one day while trying to help Chennault prove a theory. Instead of a rolling dive away from an attacker, Chennault suggested a half loop with a roll-out on top, the Immelmann. With Cannon and another pilot, Don Stace, Chennault went aloft to try it. He flew a Spad, as did Stace. Cannon took up a British SE-5.

Cannon, at a signal, dived on the other two planes, and Stace and Chennault quickly hauled back on their sticks and zoomed upward. In the midst of the maneuver, Stace changed his mind and fell out of the Immelmann into a tight spiral. Cannon's SE-5 crashed against the Spad. A grim tragedy appeared to be in the making as bits and pieces of plane wings flew and the planes limped earthward, but both pilots survived.

The unfortunate accident served merely to reinforce the veterans' conviction that their time honored methods were best, and it clamped a temporary brake on Chennault's efforts to prove the oldsters wrong.

Chapter 5

In 1923, at the age of thirty, the ex-Louisiana school teacher was given his first command, the 19th Pursuit Squadron in Hawaii. He learned many things during his tour of duty in the Islands, including a realistic understanding of the geopolitics of the Far East.

Never had he been more pleased with a tour of duty than in flower-scented Hawaii. He spent long hours flying as co-pilot in the bombers, towing targets for ground gunners. He was in perfect physical condition, tanned and lean, and now sporting, as he put it, "a fierce black mustachio."

Despite the seriousness with which Chennault approached his work, it was not all drudgery and tiresome routine in Oahu. One day while the 19th was patrolling, they spotted a string of anti-aircraft batteries neatly lined up on the beach, blazing away at Al Hegenberger who was flying back and forth towing the white target sleeve behind his plane. Chennault, never passing up an opportunity to inject realism into practices he sometimes considered nonsense, decided to give the flak gunners a taste of what they could look forward to in a real war.

Waggling his wings, he led the whole squadron in a dive-bombing attack on the flak guns. Pulling out over the beach, Chennault leaned out of his cockpit to laugh at the baldheaded colonel in command scuttling for cover along with the surprised battery crews. At a height of a hundred feet he chased the colonel up and down the sandy beach, leaning out of the cockpit to laugh at him.

When the planes returned to their Ford Island base, the airfield was in an uproar. Headquarters was irate. Chennault asked an officer innocently, "Any idea who did it?"

"No," the base commander replied angrily, "but the artillery colonel says it was that damned Frenchman with the big black mustache! Why—you—"

The commander of the 19th Squadron was confined to the post for a week.

With the passing of the 1924 Immigration Act that practically excluded Japanese from the United States, a mild war scare flared in the Pacific. Japanese War Lords shouted for war, and as the tension built up during the next year, Hawaiian Island military stations, particularly Chennault's air group, maintained emergency conditions. Lieutenant Chennault had not needed orders calling for extreme vigilance, for the vulnerability of this Pacific outpost to a sneak attack had long been uppermost in his mind. The longer he stayed in Hawaii the more convinced he became of the growing importance of events in the Far East to American security; the more probable it seemed that one day soon Japan would make her bid for domination of the Pacific. Fifteen years later she did just that.

One hot afternoon he called his pilots and ground

crew chiefs into the Luke Field Operations hut. His usual dry smile was missing, and they sensed something special was brewing as his dark eyes swept over them.

"Gentlemen, I have called this meeting because we have new orders. You've all read the statements of the Japanese military leaders, and you know what a prize Pearl Harbor represents. If the Japs should go to war every one of us knows we'll be the first target they'll try to hit . . . She'll strike from the air and she won't serve notice . . . From right now, the 19th Pursuit Squadron will operate as if attack may come at any minute, and I tell you now it can very well happen. We won't wait for scheduled takeoff time for this afternoon's patrol. Take off immediately when we finish here!"

Pilots rose to go, and Chennault snapped them back into their seats. "Beginning tomorrow this squad will be in the air at four-thirty a.m. I mean in the air. You will fly with full loads of ammunition, machine guns tested and ready to shoot, and if the enemy appears you will attack."

He stared at the pilots as he had stared at the rowdy school kids back in Athens, Louisiana, searching for signs of even mild rebellion. He smiled, and nodded. "I don't know what the other squadrons will do, but I know the 19th won't get caught on the ground if the Japs come hunting. That's all, and thank you."

Next morning in the pre-dawn mists blanketing the field, the 19th Pursuit Squadron became airborne, pilots alert and looking for a fight. For six straight weeks Chennault kept the squadron on emergency alert patrol, his fighters circling the Islands, listening for the thunder of Japanese bomber engines sixteen years too soon.

When a few of the pilots, chafing at the monotony, tried to get extra winks of sleep, Lieutenant Chennault came into the barracks and pulled them forcibly out from under their blankets, using his saltiest Texas vocabulary to get them onto the field and into their planes. Gradually, the tension eased, sabres stopped rattling in Japan, and vigilance relaxed. Supply officers sighed with relief when Chennault finally announced the emergency was over, and shook their heads when they checked the amount of gasoline left on the field.

In later years, Claire Chennault said sadly, "The Japanese threatened war then that they never carried out. That was in 1925, but anyone who knew history should have known the Japanese threat would have to be carried out someday and required more alertness on our part year by year.

"Had I been in Pearl Harbor in December 1941, I certainly would have had my men in the air then, too."

The record shows that after Chennault reached China and saw the Japanese in action there, he became convinced that a sudden Japanese attack somewhere in the Pacific, probably at Pearl Harbor, was becoming increasingly imminent, and he so warned his Government more than once in the months preceding Pearl Harbor. The warnings were not heeded.

With Hegenberger, Chennault sincerely believed trans-Pacific ferry flights from the U. S. mainland to Hawaii could be routine, obviating shipments of planes by boat that wasted valuable time. Together they checked estimated gas consumption, point-to-point distances on a specified route, and time-in-flight. Finally putting aside their slide-rules, they deemed such a flight was practical, settling on a tri-motored Fokker for the job. Putting it all on paper they forwarded it to the top brass for a try. It was rejected as impractical.

A year later, however, while Chennault listened near a radio at Brooks Field in Texas, Lester Maitland and Hegenberger successfully flew the Fokker over the designated route.

Thoroughly sold on the idea of holding a formation together during the acrobatics of combat, concentrating its firepower, rather than spreading out all over the sky in individual dogfights, Chennault inveigled two of his most conservative pilots into what seemed casual discussions of the theory. Finally they bit at his bait and suggested they try it out. They practiced "behind closed doors," and then staged a show over Luke Field that was so successful that the rest of the squadron joined in the experiments.

The first formation attack completely befuddled the Navy. Off Oahu, Chennault's squadron spotted a squadron of Vought dive bombers high above them, simulating an attack on Pearl Harbor.

The Navy pilots figured the defending Air Corps planes were too low to attack and streaked on toward their target. All of the 19th fighter planes simultaneously pulled up into an Immelmann formation that brought them on the tail of the Navy bombers, then roared with opened throttles through the Voughts without breaking formation. One Navy pilot was so startled he spun out of formation.

"If the shooting had been for keeps," Chennault jubilantly told his pilots upon landing, "we would have wiped them out before they knew what hit them."

Chapter 6

Back at Brooks Field in Texas, following his tour of duty in Hawaii, Chennault and two other men began looking for workable techniques by which to carry out an idea originally suggested by Brigadier General Billy Mitchell—paratrooper operations.

They practiced a V-formation of planes dropping men and infantry equipment until the paratroopers were opening fire with air-dropped machine guns in less than a minute after their feet touched the ground.

Two infantry officers who observed and were impressed by the first air drop demonstration staged by Chennault were later to serve with him in China: Colonel Fred C. Milner, as Adjutant General of the Fourteenth Air Force, and Major General Charles B. Stone, who succeeded Chennault as commanding general of the 14th Air Force.

Other American defense chiefs were less than electrified although they had just witnessed the birth of the paratroops. German and Russian military observers, however, saw it differently. A few weeks later, a Russian military mission rolled onto the field, and sought out Chennault. They presented him with cases of vodka, chocolate, and caviar before offering him a job developing paratroops in their country. "I'm a fighter pilot," Chennault told the Russian in charge. "This paratrooper business is just a sideshow."

"Think it over," the Russian said, "let us know."

Chennault's decision was not easy. He had been more than eight years in the American Army, a first lieutenant drawing $225 a month, including flying pay, plus rations, and quarters for his family. Above all, he was aching for a chance to prove his theories. His curiosity aroused, he wrote Amtorg, the Russian trading firm, demanding what he considered exorbitant terms: a five-year contract, $1,000 a month, plus expenses, the rank of Colonel, and the right to fly any plane in the Red Air Force.

The reply set him back on his heels. "When can you leave?"

He was an excellent poker player and he had to admit they had called his bluff, but the Russians grew tired of writing letters that were never answered. He still hoped his own country would undertake such a program, but until long afterward it did not.

In peacetime, promotions come slowly. It was eight and a half years after he had received his commission in September, 1920, that he reached the rank of Captain on April 12, 1929. By then he was widely known as "that radical Chennault" for his advanced theories of military aviation.

The top command of the Air Corps had decided that the heyday of the pursuit plane was over and had relegated pursuit aviation to a distinctly secondary role. This was the era of belief in the invincibility of the heavily-armed bombardment airplane. One voice —that of Captain Chennault—disagreed violently.

Unable to convince his superiors that with improved methods of early detection and warning, fighter planes could intercept and destroy attacking bomb-carrying planes, no matter how heavily armed, Chennault as early as 1923 began sending his views, in the form of well-reasoned articles, to the service magazines.

Even editors proved skeptical. Invariably, Chennault's articles were preceded by a notice stating that the views of the author did not necessarily coincide with those of the magazine or of the Air Corps. Reading this material today, it is difficult to understand why for so many bitter, frustrating years, Claire Chennault's was a lone voice crying in the murky wilderness of unheeding officialdom.

I can only conclude that the General's great friend, Tom Corcoran, was right when he said: "Chennault suffered from 'genius trouble'. The trouble any genius faces is that there just aren't enough other geniuses around to know what in the hell the genius is talking about! They conclude, therefore, that he is not a genius at all, but a crackpot."

I fear that it has always been this way—since the dawn of human history—that men of great vision must inevitably encounter inertia, blindness, and determined opposition. What is so crystal clear to such men remains formless and obscure to many of their contemporaries. Some men of vision grow silent and embittered and resigned. Their voices fade, their spirits quail under the avalanche of derision and criticism. They see no way through the thick viscous walls of official intertia. A few, convinced of the rightness of their vision, and caring enough, persist. They continue indomitable missionaries of their convictions, doggedly seeking to implant what they see as right in the minds of those who have the power to decide. Only death can silence such spirits and sometimes their voices continue to be heard from beyond the grave.

For long years, Claire Chennault worked far into the night on his articles in the hope they would produce action on his theories. But, although they are now deemed to have been written persuasively and with great clarity, no one, apparently, understood.

Again and again, he preached a fighter plane strategy of "Detection, interception, destruction," and in 1935 he published his brilliant and prophetic "The Role of Defensive Pursuit." Its basic precepts are as valid today in the defensive use of radar, jet and rocket-powered missiles as they were in 1935 for the fighter planes of that day.

Claire Chennault's theory rested in large measure on the first of his three basic principles—detection: the establishment of an early warning system so that planes could take off with a fairly clear idea of where the approaching enemy planes could be intercepted and destroyed. Today, with our early warning radar nets in constant operation, such as the Dew line, the need for such a system seems obvious. But this basic defense need was completely unrecognized by American air strategists in the 1930's. It remained for Claire Chennault to prove his theories by establishing the famous Chinese air warning net in July of 1937 in the Shanghai, Hangchow, Nanking triangle to protect the capital, Nanking. This net was followed by the other later ones set up by his communications officer, John Williams, which gave the Flying Tigers a tremendous advantage over the Japanese Air Force in China to the end of World War II.

Chennault always welcomed good ideas, from whatever source, and one of his firmest beliefs was in the theories originally developed by an early German flying ace. Oswald Von Boelcke had discovered that two planes could be flown in unison, to fight together as a team. This fact he coupled with another: "The difference between the firepower of two opposing forces, other factors being equal, is the square of the difference of the number of fire units. Thus, two planes, flying as a team, and attacking a single enemy plane, enjoyed odds not of two to one, but of four to one." I do not, myself, understand this clearly, but I quote from the General's papers verbatim, and I understand that this is today a well accepted fact.

Von Richtofen, the German World War I ace, had earlier demonstrated the validity of Von Boelcke's theory. His Flying Circus was never defeated by Allied airmen until Hermann Goering took command. He led the Circus back into individual dogfight tactics and it was decimated.

During this waiting period Chennault was senior

Generalissimo Chiang Kai-shek shakes hands with Gen. Chennault, after presenting him with a medallion signifying the highest honor ever paid a foreigner by the Chinese government. The award is titled "The Order of the Blue Sky and White Sun."

Part of the American Volunteer Group in San Francisco, on way to China. July, 1941.

Luke Williamson, one of the "Three Men on the Flying Trapeze" and later Gen. Chennault's personal pilot in China and Commanding Officer of 14th Air Force transport squadrons.

instructor in fighter tactics at the Air Corps Tactical
School, Maxwell Field, Alabama. He was trying, above
all, to emphasize team-work fighting according to
planned tactics as the fundamentals of all fighter
plane action. This concept was lost on many; in
fact, some of his fellow officers regularly recommended
that the fighter course be scrapped. But Chennault
found a friend in Major General John F. Curry, Commandant of the Tactical School, who firmly rejected
all such suggestions.

At Captain Chennault's suggestion, General Curry
authorized the formation of an Air Corps acrobatic
team of three expert flyers. The purpose was to test
Chennault's theory that what one plane could do in
aerial acrobatics, three or more could also do, provided the pilots were skilfull enough to perform the
maneuver simultaneously.

The team was picked by inviting all candidates to
stick on Chennault's tail for thirty minutes of violent acrobatics. The two best were Lieutenants S. H.
Hansell and J. H. Williamson. Williamson was later
to precede him to China and would, still later, become his personal pilot. The three went up in P-12
pursuit ships, fast, trim biplanes which were highly
maneuverable. There was no inter-plane radio communication in those days and the pliots depended on
hand signals from the leader.

The trio, calling themselves "Three Men on a Flying Trapeze," performed every acrobatic maneuver
known—loops, chandelles, Immelmanns, slow rolls,

double rolls—and some that weren't known, always in perfect formation. In one routine to prove the precision of pilots and planes, they tied the aircraft together with 20-foot lengths of light rope. They would take off, twist and turn through incredible acrobatics, and land with the rope intact. It took perfect timing and coordination and if one pilot made even a slight mistake, the others had to slip into the faulty maneuver to keep from snapping the rope. They were forerunners of famous precision flying teams of today, such as the "Blue Angels."

Although the team received many official commendations and civilian trophies, few seemed to realize that the "Three Men on a Flying Trapeze" was not just a stunt, but proof of Boelcke's theory that fighter planes flying in unison could bring their combined fire power continuously to bear on a single target throughout most violent of combat maneuvers.

In the Cleveland Air Races in 1934, Lt. W. E. "Billy" MacDonald replaced Lt. "Possum" Hansell as a team member. In January of 1936 the team of Chennault, Williamson and MacDonald staged a farewell performance at the Pan-American air maneuvers in Miami. Among the spectators was General Mow Pang Tsu of the Chinese Air Force, a man they would all see again under far different circumstances.

As the fame of the Flying Trapeze spread through the flying world, letters began to arrive from Roy Holbrook, an ex-Air Corps pilot then a flying instructor in China. Holbrook asked Chennault to recommend a dozen American pilots for the Chinese Air

Force flying school in Hangchow, south of Shanghai. Among those he recommended were J. H. "Luke" Williamson and Billy MacDonald. They sailed for China in the summer of 1936.

In the same year, Claire Chennault's health began to fail. Only a man with an iron constitution could have stood his daily schedule during the preceding five years. His work as flying instructor began at dawn. He served on a number of boards, including the Air Corps Board and the Pursuit Design Board, conducted daily precision flying drills, took part in field maneuvers and, meanwhile, battled the proponents of the "invincible bomber" in endless arguments.

Night after night he burned midnight oil writing his articles for the service magazines. In five years at the Tactical School he had not a single day of leave and for several years his chronic bronchitis had been growing worse as he pushed himself unsparingly. Most of the winter of 1936 he spent in a hospital bed in Hot Springs, Arkansas.

But he still dreamed of his flying theories and of ways to prove them. He knew this could only be done by putting them into practice; and this, unfortunately, seemed to require a war. He began to read more thoughtfully the letters that kept coming from China.

With his usual farsightedness, it seemed to Claire Chennault—as it had seemed to him in Hawaii—that full-scale war between China and Japan and between the United States and Japan was inevitable. For years

Japan had been clawing away at North China and he felt these small-scale forays were merely preliminary to an all out Japanese attack.

China was frantically trying to prepare for resistance. Individual Americans, Russians, Italians, and other Occidentals were already in China, hired to train Chinese airmen. But graft and corruption were draining vitality from the program and the fledgling Chinese Air Force was suffering from rivalry between American and Italian advisors. In the spring of 1937, brilliant and determined Madame Chiang Kai-shek personally took on the task of eliminating the graft and building an effective Air Force.

Soon after Claire Chennault's release from the hospital, Madame Chiang through Roy Holbrook sent Chennault an offer too attractive to refuse. It offered Captain Chennault a three-month contract to make a confidential inspection of China's young air force, and permission to test-fly any plane in the Chinese Air Force.

With that letter fate knocked on Claire Chennault's door. Forty-four years old and, for the moment, tired of struggling, he had reluctantly come to the conclusion that his Army career no longer held promise. The Army, suggesting retirement for deafness, appeared to agree. Although he knew he was no deafer than many other flyers who had spent thousands of hours in noisy open cockpits, on April 30, 1937, without argument, he accepted retirement.

On the following day he left Louisiana bound for San Francisco and China.

Part **2** *The Challenges*

"One should not be bound by fixed rules of conduct but vary his plans according to the requirements of the enemy with the sole object of winning a decisive victory."

THE ART OF WAR—SUEN WUU

(155-220 A.D.)

Chapter 7

When the President Garfield docked at Kobe, Japan, late in May of 1937, Claire Chennault went quietly ashore for a warm reunion with Billy MacDonald who was waiting on the dock.

"How is it an instructor in the Chinese Air Force can move about freely in Japan?" Chennault asked.

Billy grinned. "You're mistaken, Major! I'm an assistant manager of a troupe of acrobats. See, it says so right here in my passport. I ditched the troupe in Osaka and came here to meet your ship. For the next few days you and I are going to be 'tourists'—like the Japanese tourists that wander around the U.S. Ever noticed them?"

Chennault nodded grimly. "Especially around harbors and airfields."

"We'll return the compliment!"

The two friends hired a car and for several days toured Japan with cameras concealed beneath their topcoats. Through the eyes of experienced airmen they gazed at potential bombing targets, new building construction, industrial centers, shipping points and shipping bottlenecks. They used their cameras often, right under the noses of the secret police, and then sailed for Shanghai.

Their pictures turned out well but were only a start toward an effective target briefing manual. To his surprise, Chennault found out four years later that his pictures and notes contained more information useful to him on Japanese targets than the War Department's official files.

Shanghai still showed traces of the 1931 Sino-Japanese fighting, although the threat of war was not being taken seriously in the bars and elegant clubs of the "Paris of the Orient."

Soon after his arrival, Chennault was driven by Roy Holbrook to the high-walled compound in the French concession to meet his new employer, Madame Chiang Kai-shek.

She looked much younger than he had expected. He was completely captivated and she was instantly impressed with him. Both spoke in soft Southern accents, Madame Chiang having been educated in Georgia.

"I reckon you and I will get along all right in building up your air force," he told her after some discussion.

"I reckon so, Colonel," she drawled in return.

That night he wrote in his diary: "She will always be a Princess to me."

On that hot sticky day in Shanghai, Madame Chiang became serious. She wanted plain, unvarnished facts concerning the Chinese Air Force and she wanted them in a hurry. She suggested that Chennault begin at Nanking.

Without delay Chennault and Billy MacDonald picked up two Douglas biplanes at the Hangchow

Flying School and once more his hand was on a throttle and it was good to be in the air again looking down at the rich green rice paddies.

At Nanking, Chennault found that what he'd heard in Shanghai was true. The Chinese pilots were as unready to take to the air as the planes were unready to fly, despite the fact that an Italian training mission at considerable cost to China had been at work for some time operating a training school and an assembly plant. The orders rolled in but the assembly plant was turning out obsolescent airplanes—and the training school for pilots was in the habit of graduating every socially prominent young man on his rolls whether he could fly or not.

Chennault now embarked on an inspection trip of the entire Chinese Air Force and its installations, hoping he would find conditions better elsewhere than in Nanking. But his inspection trip was never completed nor did he ever write the expected report to Madame Chiang Kai-shek, for at this juncture, the Japanese took a hand. On the night of July 7, 1937, Japanese soldiers marched over the Marco Polo Bridge about 15 miles southwest of Peking and paused on the threshold of the village of Wanping. They announced that one of their men was missing and that they must therefore search Wanping. The town magistrate refused, for this was an old maneuver to him. By similar deception, the Japanese had already slipped into five provinces and had forced the demilitarization of a portion of Hopei Province.

Shortly after midnight troops of the Chinese 29th Army clashed with the Japanese forces at the Bridge and at Wanping. To the surprise of the Japanese, the 29th Army did not quit but bravely hurled its 10,000 poorly equipped troops against double that number of Japanese soldiers. The news shook the world, for this had all the earmarks of something far more serious than an international "incident." News of the Japanese attack reached Colonel Chennault and Billy MacDonald while they were still on their inspection trip, and from the Italian Flying School at Loyang Chennault sent a telegram to Generalissimo Chiang Kai-shek who was in the mountain resort of Kuling. Chennault offered his services in any capacity in which they could best be used. Later on he gave three reasons for his action:

1. I never run from a fight.

2. After all the years of classroom argument and theoretical debate over my theories of warfare, I wanted a chance to give them an acid test in combat.

3. I was convinced that the Sino-Japanese War would be a prelude to a great Pacific war involving the United States. I felt that the more I could learn about the Japanese and the more damage I could inflict in the early stages on the conflict, the better I would be able to serve my country eventually.

Two days later the answer came in the form of a telegram from the Generalissimo:

Your voluntary offer of services gratefully accepted. Proceed to Nanchang. Direct final combat trainer fighter groups there.

This telegraphic exchange launched Claire Lee Chennault upon his most fantastic adventures as an aviator. In Nanchang, famous, as he said, for exquisite porcelain and sweltering heat, he found that his staff consisted of General P. T. Mow of the Chinese Air Force, Billy MacDonald and himself and a few of the poorly Italian-trained Chinese pilots, most of whom could not fly. The available equipment included a group of Curtiss Hawk-3 biplanes, a group of Hawk-2 biplanes and a third group of Fiats and Boeing P-26's.

In his private papers, Chennault wrote: "Combat training at Nanchang was a positive nightmare. Fighter pilots supposed to be combat-ready crashed and killed themselves in basic trainers. On a muddy field we'd have as many as five landing crack-ups in a day."

Claire Chennault, General Mow and Billy Mac-Donald began the difficult job of making qualified fighter pilots out of the eager, potentially well-qualified Chinese boys whom the Italians had failed to train properly. It was difficult, exhausting and exasperating work. The hot summer sun burned the Chinese plains brown and heat waves danced in the dusty streets. The temper of the Chinese people waxed as hot as the weather. Hawkers sold gas masks. Students chanted and demonstrated. Roof tops were camouflaged with gray paint. The press headlined "Stand and fight. It is better to be broken jade than whole tile."

China's national war fund grew from "one day's pay" contributions from the teeming millions. Never before so united, China was building toward her hour of crisis. In his summer capitol on the slope of Kuling —the mountain of the Ox—Generalissimo Chiang Kai-shek felt the weight of the decision that was his— whether to take 500,000,000 people into the hell brew of modern warfare or back down to Japanese arrogance and insults. He and his generals took stock of their tools of war and shook their heads. They had the highest ranking admiral in the world's navies—and a few old rusty gunboats. They had one crack Army of 80,000 and an untried Air Force scarcely five years old. Japan had a new immensely powerful Pacific Navy and a large air fleet of thousands of planes copied accurately from the world's best airplanes. She had millions ready for conscription and her material resources were great.

The Generalissimo decided to check on his Air Force; Chennault and General Mow were summoned to report at once to Kuling. General Mow seemed to know what was coming. Sweat broke out on his forehead as they approached the Generalissimo's residence and he stood stiffly at attention as the Generalissimo asked the fateful question, "How many first-line planes are ready to fight?"

"Ninety-one, Your Excellency" replied Mow in a firm voice, but his face was pale.

Chennault later described the scene as follows:

"Chiang turned red and I thought he was going to explode. Color drained from Mow's face as he stood stiffly at attention, his eyes fixed straight ahead.

"Never in the eight years that I have known him have I seen the Generalissimo so mad. As his anger ebbed, he turned and asked in Chinese: 'What does your survey show?'

" 'General Mow's figures are correct', I replied."

The Generalissimo continued to pace but some of the anger and strain left his face and Chennault told him the truth, all of it. In doing so he established the basis of an intimacy with General Chiang which no other non-Chinese has ever approached. This liaison was later to serve him well when official Chinese red tape had to be unsnarled in a hurry.

Following the conference with Colonel Chennault, Chiang Kai-shek summoned an historic conference in the Nanking Military Academy where eight years later the Japanese would sign a formal surrender. All of the old war lords of China were there, the good ones and the bad, the arrogant and the cooperative—the current heirs of China's divided rule down through the centuries. Present was old ironsides, Pa Chung Psi, Czar of the lesser war lords of southwest China, the man to whom the Japanese once gave, free, an air force, hoping he would use it against Generalissimo Chiang Kai-shek; There were Governor Lung Yun, of Yunnan, who had only one eye; Shanshi's Governor, Yen Hsi Shan and Yu Han Mow from the Cantonese; Han Fe Chu from Shuntung Province; the well-known Christian General, Fung Yu Hsiang; elderly Ho Chien, Governor of the Hunan rice bowl area; and a number of others. Many had been enemies of Chiang Kai-shek for years; some had at times been friends and at other times enemies. Collectively, these men ruled millions of Chinese people, with life and death power over those within the territories they controlled. Always they had been jealous of each other. Now they came at Chiang's bidding not because he asked them to or because they wanted to but because China was in mortal danger and they knew that Chiang Kai-shek was the only leader among all of them who could lead them into a united defense of China.

At this historic conference Claire Chennault and Billy MacDonald were the only "foreigners." MacDonald was an adviser; Chennault the air arm of the Generalissimo. The outcome was gratifying; a great victory for the Generalissimo and for China. All agreed to fight together under Chiang. As General Chennault later said: "China was united for the first time in modern history. The watery components that had flowed first in one direction and then another were now solidly frozen into hard unyielding ice. It is a tragedy for modern China that that moment in Nanking was so brief."

On August 6, the Generalissimo, in an historic decision, announced to the people of China that China would yield no more, even if this means fighting literally to the death. The effect was electric. Throughout

China, bugles sounded, bells clanged, firecrackers exploded in immemorial custom. The streets and the lanes and the roadways filled with volunteers for China's armies. The hour of modern China had struck and Claire Chennault was in the thick of the mighty drama. No more playing at war, no more training for a war that might not come; the war had found Claire Chennault; he welcomed it; he would stay with it to the bitter end.

Chapter 8

One of the many ironical aspects of General Chennault's long early years as a prophet without honor in his own country is illustrated by what happened in China at the very outset of the Sino-Japanese War in 1937. For nearly twenty years Chennault had battled to make the U. S. Army Air Corps modernize combat tactics for the fighter airplane—and had failed so completely that the fighter plane had been practically abandoned as an air weapon, and he was retired. But, it took him only five days to convince the Japanese!

During the first five days of the fighting in the skies over China a small picked squad of Chinese fighter pilots trained by Chennault in bomber interception work, knocked fifty-four Japanese heavy bombers out of the sky during the first three Japanese air raids over Nanking.

The Chinese pilots flew in three-plane formations like the "Three Men on a Flying Trapeze." As the unescorted Jap bombers thundered in from Formosa (the Japanese base), each Chinese fighter formation selected a single bomber and hit it simultaneously from above, below and the rear. Three air regiments of Nippon's best bombers went down in flames before the Japanese agreed entirely with Chennault that fighter planes could knock down unescorted bombing planes. They never again sent unescorted bombers over China.

Colonel Chennault at Madame Chiang Kai-shek's request warned Shanghai that a Japanese attack on the city was not only possible but believed to be very imminent. Chennault went at once to the American Consulate, cooled his heels for an hour before a minor functionary heard him out, registering disbelief. No action was taken. The same treatment greeted him at the 4th Marine Barracks, at the office of the China National Aviation Corporation, and at a diplomatic tea party. Only one member of the foreign community, the Swedish Minister, took the warning seriously.

Two days afterward three Japanese cruisers in the Whangpoo River off the Shanghai Bund opened fire on the city and left much of it a shambles.

Shortly after Shanghai residents had finally realized that war in earnest had begun came a day of horror, Shanghai's famous Black Saturday. Light bombers from the Chinese Air Force, attacking the Japanese cruisers in the Whangpoo, inadvertently dropped two 1100-pound high-explosive bombs almost dead center in the most crowded section of the main thoroughfare, Nanking Road, near the Sun Company Department Store. One of the huge bombs was mercifully a dud. The other killed 950 people and wounded an additional 1,150.

On that same day Chennault came under fire in the air for the first time, ironically from machine guns on

the British cruiser Cumberland. The British thought
they were being attacked when Chennault was merely
attempting to identify the ship. Upon landing, Colonel Chennault pointed out the bullet holes in his
unarmed plane to his armament specialist, Rolfe
Watson:

"Get some guns on this ship and get 'em on in a
hurry. Next time anybody shoots at me I'm going to
shoot back!"

During the following months Chennault would
have plenty of opportunities to use his new guns and
would take full advantage of every opportunity. In
fact, quite unofficially but equally authoritatively, he
appears to have been not only the most unheralded
flying ace of World War II but also the most outstand-
ingly successful. On reliable authority he is generally
credited with having single handedly shot down in
the murky skies over China not less than 40 Japanese
aircraft.

However, he soon discovered that most of his
troubles were likely to be administrative. Although
well prepared for the coming combat, he was not at
all prepared for a host of unexpected problems that
at once confronted him—pilots who refused to bail
out of stricken planes because to come back without
the plane meant loss of face . . . constructing runways
without engineers or machinery . . . a headquarters
that needed two days to write air combat orders, with
each copy laboriously hand brushed . . . teaching artillery men who had never bagged ducks on the wing

to lead a moving target . . . saving from firing squads the lives of pilots who had inadvertently disobeyed orders—the enemy was killing them fast enough without any help from the Chinese.

These problems had to be faced and solved by a man without any command power. Chennault's title was and remained that of Adviser to the Secretary of the Commission for Aeronautical Affairs, Madame Chiang Kai-shek. Chennault never had legal status as a belligerent, although he was, technically, a Colonel in the Chinese Air Force. However, he actually enjoyed real authority. Frequently, he directed combat operations of the Chinese Air Force by simply making "suggestions." Few questioned his suggestions. Those who did soon found that these had the full force and effect of an order. Frequently, these "suggestions" were reenforced in writing by Generalissimo Chiang Kai-shek. Sometimes the endorsement would carry the words "without fail." It was much later that Colonel Chennault discovered that the words "without fail" meant strict compliance with the "suggestions" —or the firing squad.

To add to his difficulties, the United States Department of State issued requests, followed by stern warnings, for all American flyers to leave China, acting on demands from the Japanese who had been stung by their initial air losses over Nanking. Some Americans left China but others, including Chennault, remained. Through mutual friends, he informed the American Consul-General in Shanghai that he would be de-

lighted to leave China—after the last Japanese had
left. Finally the threat that a U. S. sheriff would be
sent to deport him under guard made Chennault reluctantly conclude that a few precautions had best
be taken. After this he officially disappeared from
time to time, with the aid of numerous friendly American officials and a few cleverly executed diplomatic
maneuvers on the part of his Chinese friends.

In view of the rather pitiful state of her defenses,
China chalked up some remarkable successes at the
outset of the war. A few nights after the terrible mistake in the bombing raid on the cruisers, a night
fighter squadron trained for the job by Chennault
pounded three 500-pound bombs onto the decks of
the Japanese cruiser Idzumo. Japanese tugs pulled the
burning ship out to sea before dawn broke. Oddly,
the Idzumo returned to her Whangpoo moorings off
the Bund three days afterwards looking fresh and apparently unmarked. The maneuver did not fool the
Chinese who merely chalked it up to "face saving"
on the part of their enemy. Events proved this to be
correct. After the war, the record shows the Idzumo
sunk in the mud considerably away from the Whangpoo but revealed no trace of an identical sister ship.

On the defensive front, another Chennault spe-
cialty, the air raid warning net, helped to protect the
vital Shanghai-Hangkow-Nanking triangle. After the
Marco Polo bridge affair one of Chennault's suggestions endorsed by the Generalissimo with the words
"without fail" made all telephone and telegraphic

facilities in that area available for early warning pur-
poses. After this, no enemy could approach a target
by surprise.

The Chinese air net was the start of the greatest
single key to Chennault's aerial success in China. At
the time of its inauguration the weak Chinese air defenses could do little to prevent the destruction of
ground targets. However, hundreds of thousands of
Chinese lives were saved by the net's operations, because once the bugles blew and the sirens sounded and
the air alert was out, people scurried for cover and
were saved. Later, it was the means by which American fighters were to decimate the Japanese Air Force.
"Forewarned is forearmed"—and never before had
this been proved so completely. Once again the tactics
which Chennault had labored vainly to have placed in
effect by the U. S. Army proved their worth in the
battle-torn skies over China. It was merely one more
in a long string of vindications of Chennault's genius
and foresight.

But because of the small number of Chinese planes
and the unpreparedness of the pilots, the end of the
Chinese Air Force was inevitable. In October, the
Japanese bombers returned to Nanking protected by
scores of new heavily armed fighter planes and by the
end of October hardly a dozen of the original 80-odd
Chinese planes were left and a large proportion of the
Chinese pilots were dead.

Claire Chennault, however, and his new fast mono-
plane, a Curtiss-Wright-Hawk special were in excel-

lent condition. The Hawk soon became the best known and deadliest in the Chinese Air Force. It was at that time by far the fastest plane in the skies over China and its work as a reconnaissance plane was so effective that an entire Japanese fighter group based near Shanghai was ordered to concentrate on downing the Hawk. They failed. For more than ten months Chennault's special roamed China's skies, a period far longer than the normal operating life of Chinese airplanes in the Sino-Japanese War. It finally crashed while being flown by a test pilot after a repair job.

The Hawk became known as the U. S. Army Air Corps P-36. It demonstrated the sharp difference between the United States and Japanese concept of air warfare. The Japanese were constructing planes that where lightly armored, extremely maneuverable, and intended to be expendable. The Japanese believed it was easier to produce complete new planes in Japan and move them to the front to replace those that were damaged, than become involved in cumbersome field repair operations. The same theory of expendability extended to the pilots. It was better, the Japanese reasoned, to replace pilots killed because of the absence of protective armor than to armor the planess and thereby slow their flying speed.

The American approach was heavier, more rugged, better armored planes which had to be repaired and patched by ground crews, since there were no replacements available. The greater weight of the American planes made them less maneuverable. It was suicide, Chennault quickly found, to try to out-maneuver a Japanese plane in the so-called dogfight tactics which up to this time had been so much in vogue.

Chennault quickly arrived at a tactical conclusion which events over the next few years proved correct. The only way to defeat the light, fast, Japanese ma-neuverable plane was to use the high-speed diving ability of the heavier U.S. plane, making diving passes at the Jap planes and racing away. It was in his Hawk special that Colonel Chennault developed the "one pass and dive away" technique which later provided so many air victories for the members of the American Volunteer Group.

After the fall of Nanking a part of the Chinese Government moved to Hankow but this was a tempo-rary move and the Chinese high command soon se-lected Chungking, the capital of Szechwan Province 2,000 miles to the west, as the wartime capital of China. Chungking quickly became known as the most bombed city in the world. It was the bastion from which the long, hard Sino-Japanese War was fought. It was in the planning of this heroic 2,000 mile retreat to the hills that Claire Chennault first came to appreciate the implacable determination of the Chinese to resist at all costs Japan's attempt at domination.

In Hankow the Chinese Air Force under Chen-nault's leadership made a dogged last stand against the steadily swelling weight of the Japanese ground and air force in China. The battles over Hankow virtually killed off the last of the Chinese pilots who had been available at the beginning of the war. It became obvious that if China were to continue fighting, she would have to build a new air force from the ground up. Desperately trying to get planes into the air against Japanese shipping operations, Chennault bought some slow but long-range Vultee bombers and hired an "international squadron" consisting of four French, three American and one Dutch and one German pilot. Six of the best remaining Chinese bomber pilots made up the rest of the squadron. This international crew made several successful raids on bridges and rail centers and with this encouragement Chennault planned a major assault against a key Japanese troop movement center in Shantung Province. On the day before the scheduled raid, bombs and gas were loaded—and that afternoon the Japanese struck. A string of 100 pound bombs exploded along the flight line and the international squadron's planes disappeared in a series of flaming explosions.

This Japanese coup underlined the desperate plight of China. Canton, China's most important southeastern seaport, fell at about the same time that Hankow succumbed, and shortly afterward all east China was gone, with Hainan Island. Chennault's affection for Generalissimo and Madame Chiang grew when he added up the terrifying losses sustained by China at the end of two years of resistance. These added up as follows: eleven provinces; all key railroads; the Yangtze and Pearl Rivers, China's main water arteries; approximately 95% of all Chinese industry; the capital and all centers of industry, finance, and raw materials; the best divisions of the army; eventually all of the Air Force.

"Yet," commented General Chennault later, "China continued to fight and only a few had any thoughts of surrendering."

Leaving the hopeless air operation and hard fought ground battle of the Yangtze River Valley, Chennault moved the scene of his activities to Kunming in the summer of 1938. Here, on the edge of a flat green air field between Lake Kunming and the city, he set up a new training school in a renewed effort to provide China with an air force. As usual, he found the going heavy. He had looked forward to concerning himself with training and tactical air problems and found that no semblance of supply or maintenance organization had been established. Since these were necessary components to air power he had to build these too.

It was at this period that his quick American temper and the equally mercurial temper of his "boss lady"—as he affectionately called Madame Chiang Kai-shek, flared. Sometimes Chennault felt he was making no progress and he finally discovered a technique for handling Madame Chiang. Approaching her, instead of opening a string of angry complaints, he would hang his head and tell her he had come to submit his resignation. "Tell me what the trouble is," Madame Chiang would say, whereupon Chennault would give the details of his biggest current headache. His resignations seemed to average almost one a week . . . but the Chinese Air Force steadily improved.

Meanwhile, however, Japan's large scale bombing program to crack Chinese resistance in every population center of China was launched. There was nothing yet ready in the skies to stop the Japanese and the darkest days of the long war began.

Chapter 9

With time, Chennault could have given China the skilled air force it needed. But time was running out. As the Japanese, drawing on their great resources of men and machines, poured both into China it became obvious to Chennault that not only was there no time left in which to train the Chinese, there also were not enough qualified international non-Chinese pilots in China effectively to combat the Japanese by means of an international squadron.

Early in 1939, the Japanese opened an all-out campaign of sustained bombing of all cities of any size in China, with the purpose of breaking the peoples' will to resist. Generalissimo and Madame Chiang travelled throughout China trying to instill some of their courage into the people, but things went from bad to worse and in late summer of 1940 the first new Japanese Zero planes swooped down over China. The remaining Chinese fighters were swept away and Japanese bombing planes were once again able to go wherever they wished in China. The Japanese were now throwing between 100 and 150 bombers daily against Chungking and the air training school at Kunming was being plastered daily. Chennault, and the leaders of China, knew that this simply could not continue indefinitely, stoical and heroic though the people of China had proved themselves to be.

The Generalissimo and Madame Chiang and Chennault held a council of war. It had become obvious to all of them that the only remaining chance was to secure heavy and expert outside help. All three had often thought of the possibility of obtaining planes and pilots from the United States. Of the three, Chennault was probably the most pessimistic for he realized even better than the Chiangs how deeply involved the United States was in the war in Europe. But there seemed to be little else left and finally the Generalissimo directed Chennault to go to the United States at once and try to obtain American planes and pilots.

Two days after the Generalissimo's decision had been reached Chennault was enroute to the United States with General P. T. Mow. During the three-day flight Chennault planned the operation of a Chinese-American air force. To him the mission was clear. He would have to break up the heavy and sustained Japanese bombing of Chungking and while doing so destroy so many Japanese planes and pilots that the entire bombing program would be adversely affected. He decided that he would use a four-squadron group of fighters; two for the initial assault with a third ready to go in and finish a doubtful or incomplete action. This would allow one squadron to be resting at all times, at least theoretically.

He also foresaw that he would be able to make use of an extensive network of large and small airfields inside Japanese occupied China which, with ant-like coolie labor he would be able to build and rebuild as the Japs surged back and forth in the attempts he knew would come to knock out the airfields. He knew that fighting as he must with a small force he would have to use guerrilla tactics applied to the air tactical situation. But he thought that such tactics would be as effective in the air as they had often proved to be on the ground. It seemed to him that even one-shot forays from such temporary fields might make possible the destruction of an entire squadron of Japanese airplanes.

His overall concept of the entire air campaign in China went far beyond the planned destruction of Japanese aircraft over Chinese territories. It was based even at this stage on his assumption that Japan would continue to push southward in the Pacific with Singapore, the Dutch East Indies and the Philippines as war objectives. Since Japan's war effort was almost wholly dependent upon supplies from overseas, Chennault believed that the entire contemplated southward push could be averted if he could interrupt their overseas supply lines effectively. He believed that China offered the logical launching areas for air attacks on Formosan Japanese air bases and the supply sea lines and the other arteries which fed the supplies into the Japanese war effort. Long before he reached Washington, Chennault closed his brief case of notes and began to concentrate on the main task he would face when he landed—persuading official Washington to bring the proposed American air force into existence.

His secondary mission on this 1940 visit to wartime Washington was to turn over to the Air Force detailed performance specifications of the first so-called Zero Japanese fighter planes. Shortly before he left for Washington a crashed Zero plane had been captured virtually intact and flown after receiving some repairs. The statistics were interesting and impressive to Chennault and he thought they would be to the Air Corps. The Zero could travel 322 miles per hour at cruising speed; it could climb 16,000 feet in six minutes; it carried four 7.7 machine guns; and its range was 1,100 miles with a belly tank.

When he landed he turned his data over directly to the Air Corps. But he was somehow not too surprised to find that a year later, at the time of Pearl Harbor, the Air Corps technical manuals contained a blank page in regard to the Zeros. He was getting used to this sort of thing by now. A year previously he had turned over similar data on the Japanese MIG-type 97 fighter, the predecessor of the Oscar and a plane that many American pilots rated higher in performance than the Zero. After studying this material the War Department had notified him in a letter that although it appreciated his interest they were forced to inform him that it would be impossible to build an aircraft with the stated specifications, able to perform as his intelligence indicated!

Chapter 10

As he was well aware, Claire Chennault could scarcely have chosen a worse time than the fall of 1940 for attempting to sell in the United States a proposal to release American pilots and fighter airplanes for service in the far-off, almost forgotten Sino-Japanese War.

England, America's English-speaking Ally, was fighting for her life and America's entire plane-making capacity was oriented towards trying to give the RAF pilots the planes they needed to turn back the frightening German Luftwaffe. Isolationist America could see the war in Europe as potentially threatening, but few saw any reason to give much thought to the far-away war in China. Into a Washington with its official eyes fixed worriedly and singlemindedly on Europe came Claire Lee Chennault, an ex-United States Air Corps Captain and General Mow, a Chinese General, with the rather improbable proposal that the United States provide an entire fighter air force complete with planes, pilots, mechanics and administrative staff, plus high octane gasoline and replacement parts for far-off undeclared war in the Orient.

On the evening of their arrival in Washington the two were invited by the Chinese Minister for Foreign Affairs, T. V. Soong, to a private dinner. Also attending were two trusted American friends of China who were intimately familiar with official Washington, the *Herald-Tribune* syndicated columnist Joseph W. Alsop, Jr., (who was himself later to be a Flying Tiger) and Edward Ansel Maurer, then with the *Chicago Daily News*. Ambassador Soong wanted both to hear Chennault's proposals and their opinion on official government reaction to them.

After Chennault had explained his proposal, the two newspapermen gave their opinions. Both felt that the entire idea was fantastic-sounding, bordering upon the impossible and both believed sincerely that the state of public opinion in the United States was such that if the President should approve the plan, he would be thrown out of office.

It was the usual discouraging reception that Chennault was accustomed to enduring whenever he explained his "wild" ideas and theories. Nevertheless, the following day Colonel Chennault and General Mow were given the use of an office in the D. C. headquarters of China Defense Supplies and went to work drafting the details of their proposed program. In January, 1941, they submitted their overall proposition to Dr. Soong and with more determination than hope all three began making the rounds of official Washington in an effort to obtain favorable action on their proposal for an American volunteer air force to fight in China against Japanese aggression. The initial plans proposed by these three called for 350 fighter airplanes and 150 bombers for use in 1941, with 700 additional fighters and 300 bombers to come

Gen. Chennault with his close friend, Mr. Thomas G. Corcoran, in Washington, D.C.

Gen. C. J. Chow, head of the Chinese Air Force, and
Maj. Gen. Chennault.

in 1942, along with pilots and other necessary per-sonnel. To begin, Chennault wanted a P-40 fighter group, and Hudson bombers, with pilots, and right away—these to be followed as soon as possible by more modern equipment. The startled disbelief so apparent in many of the faces of those to whom Chennault talked made him begin to feel that he might as well try to sell electric refrigerators to Eskimos. He called on Senators and Congressmen, State Department officials, and anyone else that might conceivably have any influence. Out of all of these only two influential individuals seemed to have any feeling for the problems and his proposed solution as Chennault presented it. But these were important—Frank Knox, the Secretary of the Navy, and Henry Morgenthau, Secretary of the Treasury.

It is interesting that during this visit to the United States Chennault for the second time was offered the job of Air Corps instructor at the Fort Monroe, Virginia, post artillery school, with the rank of Major. On three previous occasions his application for active duty with Army Air Corps units had been rejected.

Trying to convince Washington of the rightness of his theories for achieving air supremacy in one of the forgotten areas of the world was much like trying to punch one's way through a thick, soft, but im-penetrable foam rubber mattress.

After several weeks of these intense but discourag-ing efforts by Chennault to sell his startling ideas in official circles, Ambassador Soong supplemented him with the man whose efforts, in the General's opinion, ultimately turned the scales for the American Volunteer Group of Flying Tigers in Burma and China —Mr. Thomas G. Corcoran.

The Lend-Lease vehicle for China was China Defense Supplies, a Delaware Corporation. T. V. Soong, both Ambassador to the United States and Premier of China, and the Honorable Frederick T. Delano, uncle of President Roosevelt, were co-chairmen. Secretary Morgenthau had courageously financed it with United States funds and entrusted the organization of its U. S. personnel to Thomas Corcoran, the member of the White House brain trust known throughout the country as "Tommy the Cork." There were hundreds of things to be done in the crowded China Defense Supplies office on R Street but Soong and Delano assigned Chennault's problem to Corcoran as personal top priority. For Corcoran, the task was to his heart as well as in line of duty. I emphasize it because for Chennault it began a most fortunate association with a whole group of able younger men who time and time again during the rest of his life would back him in "miracle" after "miracle."

Corcoran's past experience exactly fitted Chennault's needs. From Harvard Law school he had been secretary to Supreme Court Justice Oliver Wendell Holmes during a Republican administration and an associate of the elite law firm of Cotton & Franklin in New York. Although a Democrat, he had come to Washington during the Hoover administration as counsel for the government bank, the Reconstruction Finance Corporation. After the 1932 election he had moved into the highest echelons of the Roosevelt administration. In China Defense Supplies he was then being groomed by Mr. Roosevelt to be Under-Secretary of the Navy for Air. He had an old familiarity and confidence with all official Washington, acquaintance with both Democrats and Republicans and he knew about money. Almost most importantly, he was a leader in the Harvard Law School group then pouring into the Washington war effort on a nonpartisan basis and he could always produce exactly the right bright young man for the most difficult assignment.

By good luck for Chennault, Corcoran was intensely interested in China. When they had been together at Harvard and later in Washington, he had been an intimate of the famous Chinese Ambassador and intellectual, Hu Shih. The senior partner of his New York law firm had died as Under-Secretary of State trying to stop the Japanese invasion of Manchuria. His own brother, David, whom he now had as president of China Defense Supplies, had been a General Motors manager in Japan when the Japanese had taken over the General Motors production for trucks for Manchuria.

Corcoran therefore knew how to talk about the Japanese-Chinese problem and had gladly taken up his assignment as counsel of the China lend-lease effort. He had manned it with young men, all later to be remarkably successful, who from that time on until Chennault's death, were to be as the General called it, his "Washington squadron"—David Corcoran, William Youngman, Whiting Willauer, James Brennan, Quinn Shaughnessy, Gordon Tweedy. Their courier line to Joseph Alsop carrying messages too hot for official communication was later to be an intelligence operation invaluable to the Flying Tigers.

After the General's death Tom Corcoran wrote me a letter in which he described his first meeting with the General:

> I met Chennault in my own apartment. For the first half hour I wondered if he were mad. He produced maps of China on which were marked the extent of the Japanese penetration and in blue what he said were 'useable Chinese air fields.' Many of these airfields were between the Japanese line of occupation on the West and the coast of China to the East. Chennault's plan of operations involved obtaining fighter airplanes and American pilots to knock down Japanese bombers, and obtaining bombers to harass Japanese shipping from Chinese airfields 'inside' the Japanese lines.
>
> These inside fields figured in all operational planning as easily as if they were outside Japan's zone of occupation.
>
> Chennault talked unconcernedly about hopping from one field to another with no feasible line of supply or communications—operations that to an amateur just beginning to taste logistics seemed impossible, even though we then thought we could use the Burma Road.

If he had left in the first ten minutes I would have written him off as a fanatic, but by the end of an hour he had explained that the 'advance' fields of which he spoke were already existent, built under his direction in the last few years by Chinese hand labor, and protected by an advanced warning net and and the incredible loyalty of the population. He talked about how loose and mired down by bad roads was the Japanese occupation; how much easier it was for the Chinese to supply the fields than for the Japanese to interdict them; how air power could supply itself for short periods; how effective was the warning net; and how the entire scheme utilized a new combination of the fierce loyalty of the population and mobility of air power.

Chennault was a born teacher—he explained enough in an hour to make me believe I was dealing with something original, whether it was genius or madness; something so original that politically it would either be lost so completely we could always explain ourselves out of it or would succeed so magnificently that it could never be challenged.

I can almost reconstruct my first report to the President, who asked:

'Has he got something?'

'Yes, he is the most original brass I have ever met. You ought to see him yourself.'

'I can't do that. Is it dangerous?'

'Of course, but less dangerous than doing nothing and losing China.'

'Is he difficult?'

'He has strong opinions—mostly about mobility— but so did Stonewall Jackson and Hannibal he's always talking about.'

'Is he manageable?'

'By you? Yes, but I wouldn't want to be his ordinary boss just because of an organization chart. This is Elizabeth's Drake—you will have to let him run the show and you run him. Do you want to see him yourself?'

'You know I can't . . . keep talking . . . don't let him quit . . . and get him around to people who won't talk.'

The General was over-grateful to me. All I ever did was listen to him when no one else would listen —and persuade—or make—others listen. Once he had a captive audience he was irresistible.

Chennault, always an expert judge of men, sensed that, with Corcoran's help, he was finally on the way to success. Instinctively he placed himself in Corcoran's capable managerial hands.

The Chennault-Corcoran association was easy. Differing in their abilities, they were temperamentally much alike; they were both almost naively incapable of believing anything was impossible and as Soong admiringly said, they would both "fight a fight through the last ditch and beyond."

Meanwhile, Chennault experienced the novel situation of having plenty of money to spend—Chinese money extended by Generalissimo through Ambassador Soong—but having nothing available to buy with it! The problem wasn't money—it was airplanes, or rather, the scarcity of airplanes.

All of the new plane production for months and months ahead was earmarked for delivery to America's European Allies.

Finally, the break came, although it was actually a compromise. Burdette Wright, a Vice President of Curtiss-Wright and an old friend of Chennault's, agreed to make available one hundred of the new model P-40's currently rolling off production lines, provided Britain would waive priority. In return, Curtiss-Wright would make up the deficiency with later model planes.

Chennault did not consider the P-40B an ideal airplane for use against the highly maneuverable Japanese aircraft, but it was much better than no plane at all. He immediately accepted Curtiss-Wright's offer and after a week managed to win British approval of the plan.

Now he turned his attention to the final but all important problem of personnel. Everywhere he went he got the same answer: planes, pilots, and mechanics could not be spared for the Chinese war effort. The Army Air Corps and the Navy's Bureau of Aeronautics echoed General Hap Arnold, Chief of the Air Corps, who said simply but with great finality that he could not spare a single staff officer without endangering the Air Corps and that he would oppose any diversion of Air Corps strength to any other country.

Roosevelt, a great friend of China but master of public opinion, realized that the year before Pearl Harbor fighting planes might be a lend-lease "garden hose" but fighting men for fighting planes were something else. Particularly he was worried that the trained American reserve pilots Chennault was asking for would have to be "mercenary" employees of a so-called commercial corporation. Those who were against Chennault's plans for any reason rubbed in this mercenary aspect by reiterating that Chennault, an American, and his American aides had served China however heroically as mercenaries. I think it is interesting that the General was always sure that one of the factors that turned the scales for the AVG in the President's mind, was of all things a poem, A. E. Housman's nobly bitter "Epitaph for an Army of Mercenaries." I have heard the General and Tom Corcoran reciting it for years but it wasn't until I heard Corcoran recite it with startling effect at a reunion of the AVG and CNAC last year in Los Angeles that I fully sensed how much that "mere poem" could have meant. Considering what the AVG later was to do for an abandoned China and a world shaken to its foundations by the first Jap successes it now sounds amazingly prophetic:

> These, in the day when Heaven was falling,
> The hour when earth's foundations fled,
> Followed their mercenaries' calling
> Took their wages and are dead.
>
> Their shoulders held the sky suspended:
> They stood and earth's foundations stay.
> What God abandoned these defended
> And saved the sum of things for pay.

The President was imaginative enough to be a poet, too.

On April 15, 1941, an unpublicized Executive Order was signed which authorized reserve officers and enlisted men to resign from the Army Air Corps, the Naval and Marine air services in order to join the American Volunteer Group in China.

Adding to the elation which Chennault felt at this state of his Washington negotiations, there occurred an incident which heartened Chennault enormously. Johnny Alison, an Air Corps Second Lieutenant, arrived at Bolling Field to demonstrate to prospective Chinese purchasers the flying qualities of the Curtiss-Wright P-40B. During a few minutes of high-speed combat aerobatics, Alison gave his audience a virtual re-run of the once-famous Chennault-led aerial team, "Three Men on a Flying Trapeze." Later Chennault said, "Alison got more out of that P-40 than anybody I saw before or after."

After Alison landed, the Chinese official spectators were smiling in approval and anticipation. Indicating the P-40, they turned to Chennault and said "We need one hundred of these."

"No" said Chennault. He turned and pointed at Lieutenant Alison. "What you need is one hundred of *these!*"

Later, Johnny Alison chalked up a brilliant combat record with Chennault in China.

Chapter 11

Early in the Spring of 1941 strange rumors circulated like wildfire among the reservists in the Army Air Corps, the Naval Service and U.S. Marine stations. They were to the effect that fabulous salaries were being offered to U.S. servicemen for duty in Burma or China fighting against the Japanese Air Force. Wanted were pilots, mechanics, radio operators, and administrative personnel, according to the stories. The bills would be paid by the Chinese Government and those who were accepted would be free from service in any branch of the United States military or naval forces.

The rumors were soon confirmed as a five-man recruiting staff organized by Colonel Chennault and authorized by President Roosevelt's executive order moved quietly from air base to air base through the Army, Navy and Marine Corps telling their wondrous stories of high pay and high adventure in the Far East.

The Chennault recruiting call was heard loud and clear by Tom Trumbull, a Lincoln, Nebraska, Navy clerk who in a long letter to me after General Chennault died in 1958 included this paragraph:

A few heard the (AVG) story and took action, each in his own way, each for his own reason. The true story of the Fying Tigers in China is the aggregate of the separate stories of the nearly three hundred men. Nearly all were youngsters who for love of adventure or hope of gain took the gamble and volunteered to serve under an unknown leader and fight for an unknown government.

Slowly, as the summer months passed, the body of the organization which later became the world famous Flying Tigers began to take shape as plane pilots, mechanics, doctors, clerical personnel, a Chaplain, and two nurses signed their contracts.

These contracts with "Camco Corporation" gave them a one-year agreement with pay ranging from $250 to $750 a month, plus travel expenses, and thirty days leave with pay, free quarters, and a $30-a-month rations allowance. Pilots received $600 a month, squadron commanders $750. Stated duties called on them to manufacture, repair and operate aircraft. There was no mention in the written contracts of a $500 bonus for every Japanese airplane destroyed. This was, however, true. The bonus was paid by the Chinese Government. In addition, each contract recruit was subject to dismissal in writing for insubordination, habitual use of alcohol or drugs, illness not incurred in the line of duty, malingering and revealing confidential information. General Chennault said in his diary that at least one man was dismissed for each of these causes except that of revealing confidential information.

Claire Chennault, right so often about so many

things, was—to an extent—wrong in his doubts about the P-40 airplane. His early misgivings over its vulnerable liquid-cooled engine and inability to compete in climbing rate and maneuverability with the light, flexible Japanese planes proved to be mild drawbacks in comparison with the many advantages the plane offered. The P-40B was heavy, fast and rugged. It was armed with two .50 caliber machine guns firing through the propellor and four .30 caliber guns mounted in the wings.

But the proof of the excellence of the P-40's for the work they were destined to do in the Burma and China skies came later. At the moment, Claire Chennault was up to his neck in a furious round of activity trying to get together everything that he would need overseas. During a single week and without losing a day's work, he made two round-trip, coast-to-coast flights. His problem now was not in obtaining money or *carte blanche*. It was in obtaining the things which the money was intended to buy. He found himself working from dawn to midnight in the R Street office of Chinese Defense Supplies where he had to prepare written requisitions for every item of equipment needed from ammunition, machine gun barrels and trucks, to razor blades, candy and paper clips. Most important were medical supplies and he loaded up heavily on these, an action which paid off later. At the time the AVG was disbanded, it was impossible to obtain priceless sulfa and other drugs anywhere else in

China. The U.S. Army Air Corps received these drugs from the AVG with heartfelt thanks.

The long working hours and intense pace finally paid off. On July 7, 1941, a bone-tired Claire Chennault met his first AVG contingent in San Francisco. On July 8, he left by air for the Far East and on the 10th of July one hundred ten pilots, about one hundred fifty mechanics, and a few supporting AVG personnel sailed aboard a Dutch liner. Just before he emplaned Chennault received a telegram from Washington informing him that President Roosevelt had approved a second AVG contingent which was scheduled to arrive in China in the following November.

The Japanese were not fooled by the passport designation of the first AVG contingent as actors, bankers, musicians, clerks and students. Hardly had their ship, the "Jaegersfontaine," embarked on the high seas, when the Japanese radio announced that the first contingent of America's volunteers had left the United States and predicted that the ship would never reach port. It did, however, convoyed by two U.S. cruisers which were relieved by a Dutch cruiser off the Australian coast for the final leg of the long voyage to Singapore and Rangoon.

Beginnings are always highly important and Chennault was well aware of this. It is doubtful, however, that at this stage of the great adventure he realized fully quite what a significant and remarkable feat he and Tom Corcoran had been able to accomplish during the months of their determined and successful efforts to win the "battle of Washington." During a European-oriented war, with all the sinews of war earmarked for the embattled European defenders of freedom, Chennault and Corcoran had been sucessfully convincing on the wisdom of siphoning off men and material for China's war in the far-off Orient, in spite of the intense and bitter opposition of powerful military men, in spite of existing contracts and pressures to send everything to European Allies in their great fight against Adolph Hitler. Their victory in Washington in the summer of 1941 was never surpassed in importance by any of the other victories which the force they had brought into being would win in the months and years that followed.

Chapter 12

My husband often spoke with grim pride of the early days of the American Volunteer Group in the jungles of Burma. Some one hundred and seventy miles from Rangoon is the city of Toungoo, population about 200,000, surrounded by the jungle. Around Toungoo is quagmire and the smell of damp, rotting vegetation. The city and everything in it is plagued by green mold, buzzing, stinging insects and torrential monsoon onslaughts. During much of each year the temperature is that of a Turkish bath.

Nevertheless, Toungoo in 1941 offered three positive advantages as an air force training base in southeast Asia. Six miles outside of Toungoo, the British had built Kyedaw Airdrome, which boasted a 4,000-foot landing strip of asphalt. In addition, up until the fall of 1941, Toungoo was not subjected to the heavy bombing attacks which the Japanese Air Force was directing daily against every important military target inside China.

In the last days of July, 1941, Claire Lee Chennault's American Volunteer Group of fighter pilots arrived in Toungoo for their final training before meeting the Japanese in air battle. Chennault had tried to engage pilots between twenty-three and twenty-eight years of age with at least three years of fighter-plane experience, but only a dozen or more of the first contingent met these standards. More than half had never seen a P-40 or flown any fighter airplane. In fact, most had received the opposite sort of flight training, having flown four-engined Flying Fortresses, Navy torpedo bombers and commercial transports. The youngest was just out of flying school; the oldest, 43, had been flying Navy fighter planes for many years.

At Toungoo, Chennault faced his usual battery of vexing problems. Although the British had leased the base to the Chinese, actual combat training was at the outset strictly prohibited. Chennault finally flew all the way to Singapore to wring permission from Air Chief Marshal Sir Robert Brooke-Popham, before his pilots were able to fire their P-40 guns at ground targets during strafing practice runs. Training had been under way for two months before London reversed its initial position and permitted real combat training work. Even then, however, the stipulation was attached that Burmese air fields could not be used as bases from which to launch attacks on either the Japanese or their Siamese allies.

There were other troubles, including the worst of all—lack of spare parts, and the rather soft physical condition of the newly arrived AVG members. Chennault immediately established a rigorous exercise program consisting of sports and walking. Chennault, the teacher and physical instructor of old, was again at work, this time under adverse conditions. The food, under a Burmese contract, was poor. There were no screens or mosquito netting to deter the eager and persistent swarms of insects. There was no outside entertainment of any sort.

Finally, and among the most serious of his problems, was the fact that the pilots he had recruited almost to a man considered themselves fully ready to step into fighter airplanes and do battle against the Japanese. They were set back on their heels when Colonel Chennault served immediate notice that not a man would be permitted to shoot a single gunburst at a Japanese plane until he had completed a stiff training and gunnery course.

Under the best conditions, in a north temperate zone, the job of getting the pilots into a state of physical and mental readiness to combat successfully the numerically superior and well trained Japanese Air Force would not have been easy. Under the conditions of heat, humidity, insects, boredom, it was plain murder. By the end of August, five pilots had quit and returned to the United States. Others would depart before the fighting started and not all of the airmen would be able to finish the rigorous fighter training course prescribed by Chennault on schedule. By December 20, when the fighting did begin there were still 25 pilots not yet ready to face the Japanese in the air. Four months later there would still be eighteen not yet ready, but despite the temptation to send the half-trained pilots against the Japanese, Colonel Chennault persisted with his rigorous training regimen. His seventeen years of U. S. Army Air Corps experience, topped by three years of active fighting against the Japanese in the skies over China, made him know beyond peradventure that his men would be killed if he were to release them to fight before they were able to handle the hot but tricky P-40 properly in battle against the highly disciplined Japanese pilots.

Here at Toungoo, for the first time Chennault was able to drive forward to a military objective in the way he believed. Not for him the spit and polish of the cadet training at Louisiana State, or the red tape-restricted operating procedures of the peacetime American Army. Discipline at Toungoo was almost non-existent on the ground. Chennault did not compel saluting although he returned a salute whenever it was volunteered. His AVG personnel could wear just about whatever they wanted to wear, including open-necked shirts. They were free to gripe as they pleased—which was most of the time—and received no reprimand for occasional roughhousing that would never have been tolerated in the formal U. S. military establishment.

Between instruction periods and in the evenings the pilots whiled away their time at poker, black jack and bridge. Each weekend a number were given leave and headed for Rangoon and such nighttime entertainment as that city afforded.

Chennault tried to run the AVG on the ground in a manner as nearly as possible approximating conditions of normal community life. He held weekly "gripe sessions" at which anyone was free to speak his mind.

All told, given the rigorous conditions of heat, humidity, poor food and the swarms of hungry insects, the freedom that the little force was given seemed to pay off. Nevertheless, military officials who occasionally dropped in for a visit obviously regarded the AVG as an undisciplined civilian mob, rather than as a military-minded air group.

Inevitably reports of this sort reached the United States and Ambassador T. V. Soong sent Chennault a cable from Washington:

REPORTS TO U.S. WAR DEPARTMENT STATE YOUR GROUP CANNOT BE READY BEFORE FEBRUARY 1942 AND WILL NOT LAST TWO WEEKS IN COMBAT. YOUR COMMENT REQUESTED.

Chennault, stung, replied tersely that his group would be ready to fight by the end of November and it would continue to fight as long as needed. Watching his still-green pilots in action, he hoped that his message would come true. Chennault believed that the conditions under which his personnel were being asked to learn and serve, justified the type of informality which he allowed. He did not, however, accord the same privilege to himself. His day was long, his work exhausting, his pace fast and furious. Nearly defenseless Kunming and the wartime capital Chungking were taking a terrible beating from arrogant Japanese raiders. Thousands of Chinese were dying under the bombings and he knew that Generalissimo and Madame Chiang Kai-shek were desperately hoping that the Chinese national will to resist would last until their final hope—his AVG—were able to take the air against the Japanese Imperial Air Force. But he knew that to send his pilots and planes into the air against the Japanese Zeroes and Nates and bombers before they were ready meant death for the pilots and disaster for the AVG.

None of the pilots was more eager for action than Chennault. He could hardly wait to put to the test his career-long theories of fair combat—theories which the United States Air Corps had rejected and for the insistent advocacy of which he had been retired from the Army. In simplest terms, his concept was that fighter airplanes with the aid of an adequate early-warning network could seek out and destroy raiding bomber planes. Now, in command of a tiny force of fewer than one hundred fighter planes and facing the impressive power of the entire Japanese Air Force he would soon have his chance to prove all of his long-cherished theories.

Except for buffing the final patina of smooth expertness to his pilots' training, Claire Chennault was now ready to take to the air against Japan. In China his air raid warning system was ready. Since the Fall of 1937 he had carefully and patiently meshed together a far-flung spider web-like early warning network of people, telephone and telegraph lines and many hundreds of portable radio sets. All told, a million or more Chinese people were already serving the network around the clock. The human web of watching eyes and listening ears spread thickly in wide paths toward centers of Japanese air power and surrounded the Kunming training center for the Chinese Air Force for a hundred miles in all directions.

Each of the watching and listening posts was in-indicated on a large map in Chinese Air Force head-quarters enabling the path of an approaching enemy aircraft to be plotted with great accuracy. The air raid warning web operated so efficiently that only once during the Sino-Japanese war and World War II, following its establishment, were enemy bombing planes able to take the Chinese by surprise. In ad-dition to protecting Chinese centers against surprise attack, the warning network on numerous occasions guided lost friendly aircraft to landings in safe ter-ritory; directed Chinese rescue parties to crashed AVG and Chinese pilots and directed Chinese intelligence operatives to crashed enemy airplanes.

Colonel Chennault brought to bear on the problem of retraining his American pilots for the air war against the Japanese not only his usual tenacity of pur-pose, but all of his skill as a natural born teacher. He divided the pre-battle training program into three phases, starting with a retraining school for teaching bomber transport pilots and other multiple-engine pilots to fly the fast-landing, single-engine P-40B fighters. While this was going on, Chennault con-ducted a seventy-two-hour blackboard and lecture course in the art of fighting and defeating Japanese aviators flying light, highly maneuverable planes.

Finally, there was a sixty-two-hour course in specialized flying and battle tactics which Chennault
monitored from a ground observation post using field
glasses. He made careful notes as he observed his men
in the air and then lectured each pilot on his
technique and mistakes when they landed.

Some pilots like Bob Neale and David "Tex" Hill
who had been flying Navy dive bombers picked up the
new fighter plane techniques quickly and easily.
Others, however, found the switch to flying the tricky
P-40's beyond their ability to master. On one terrible
morning Chennault watched his green pilots crack
up six fighter planes during landing practice. The
first AVG casualties occurred during this period. One
pilot died in a midair collision; another went to his
death in a monsoon storm and a third was killed
when his propellor went wild during a steep dive.

Equally as important as being able to fly the planes
was the way in which they had to be flown in order to
survive in the air war against the seasoned Japanese
flyers. Into the lecture portion of his course Chennault poured the stored-up knowledge of his twenty
years of flying fighter airplanes plus all that he had
learned fighting the Japanese and observing others
fight the Japanese for three years in the China skies.

Captured Japanese flying and staff manuals, translated into English, were his principal textbooks. On
the blackboard Chennault drew diagrams of all Japanese aircraft in operation over China, carefully pointing out the vulnerable areas—gas tanks, oxygen stor-

age tanks, bomb bays, etc. The students were required to redraw the diagrams from memory.

Colonel Chennault began his combat course by pointing out to his men that the aerial combat tactics that had been taught would not work in the skies over Burma. He drilled into them that they would be flying against superior forces numerically; flying ships that could not climb or maneuver as swiftly as the enemy ships and that they were furthermore beyond dollar value since they could not be replaced. "Not for a million dollars," he told them, "or five million dollars could we get an extra plane at this time. Any plane you may crack up by foolishly disregarding what you are going to learn in this course cannot be replaced for any amount of money. Not only your planes, but you yourselves are irreplaceable. You are also beyond price."

He stressed that the rugged P-40 plane, properly maneuvered, should easily outfight the lighter unarmored Japanese fighter. But the plane, he stressed, had to be handled properly. The tactics he taught them were those he had been advocating for years but which had not been accepted by the Army Air Corps.

"The fighter tactics that we are going to use out here are those we must use if we are going to stay alive. They are based on the solid fact that two planes working together as a team are far more effective than three or four planes fighting separately as individuals."

Throughout the training period he stressed teamwork and it was not always easy to convince these boys who had come along during the period following the glamorous, well-publicized individual war aces of World War I. The individual "duel in the sun" was romantic, Chennault admitted to his students, but it would be suicidal here. They grew sick and tired of hearing him stress teamwork but they finally learned that Chennault knew what he was talking about. From the translated Japanese tactical fighter manuals the American pilots learned more about Japanese tactics than any single Japanese pilot ever learned.

"Japanese pilots fly by the books and these are the books they use," Chennault told them. "Study them, and you will always be one jump ahead of the enemy. You will face Japanese pilots superbly trained in mechanical flying. They have been drilled for hundreds of hours to fly in precise formation and rehearsing each tactic in each situation they may encounter.

"They have plenty of guts but lack initiative and judgment. They go into battle with a set tactical plan always, no matter what happens. Bombers will hold their formations until they are all shot down. Fighters will always try the same tricks over and over again but God help the American pilot who tries to fight them according to their plans.

"The object of our tactics is to break up their formations and make them fight according to our style. Once the Japanese are forced to deviate from their plan they are in trouble. Their rigid air discipline can be used as a powerful weapon against them.

"You must use the strong points of your equipment against the weak points of the enemy. Each type of plane has its own strengths and weaknesses. The pilot who can turn his advantages against the enemy's weaknesses, will win every time. You can count on a higher top speed, faster dive, and superior fire power. The Jap fighters have a faster rate of climb, higher ceiling, and better maneuverability. They can turn on a dime and climb almost straight up. If they can get you into a turning combat they are deadly.

"Use your speed and diving power to make a pass, shoot, and break away. You have the edge in that kind of combat. All your advantages are brought to bear on the Japanese deficiencies. Close your range, fire, and dive away. Never stay within range of the Jap's defensive fire power any longer than you need to in order to deliver an accurate burst."

Chennault harped on the vital importance of shooting accurately and conserving ammunition. "Nobody ever gets too good at gunnery," he told them. "The more Japs you get with your first burst, the fewer there are to jump you later. Accurate fire saves ammunition. Your plane carries a limited number of bullets. There is nothing worse than finding yourself in a fight with empty guns."

Day after day, Chennault repeated his instructions until he was sure that the trainees had learned their lessons and learned them well.

"With the P-40 you can count on greater speed," he told them. "You can dive faster without tearing your wings off, and you have greater fire power. Japanese planes, on the other hand, can climb faster and have a higher ceiling. If you fight their kind of fight, the old dogfights of the Lafayette Escadrille and the Flying Circus, you're going to get killed. Use your superior speed to climb above them before you make your move. Then use your greater diving speed to make a pass at them with your throttle and guns wide open. Get in short bursts and get away. Break off and climb back for the advantage of altitude after you've gotten away safely."

He told them again and again not to underrate the Japanese pilots and this alone probably saved many of their lives. Throughout their training days they had heard the Japanese described as uncoordinated dimunitive second-rate aviators with weak eyes and thick glasses. Chennault told his men to forget all of this. The Japanese, he told them, were superbly trained. They were mechanical flyers compared to Americans with their Yankee flair for individuality, but mechanical flying, he pointed out, could be effective and dangerous when combined with expert air discipline. It could only be beaten by American initiative combined with superior judgment. The Japanese flyers would stick together under air attack longer than would be thought possible. It would be the AVG's job to break up their formations and make them fight an unfamiliar kind of fight. Then the enemy would be in trouble, being unable to improvise readily and brilliantly. "But don't ever underestimate the Japanese pilot," Chennault warned them. "He is a worthy enemy, courageous and fanatically dedicated. But his rigid air discipline can be used against him and it will be your job to do just that. Never, never—in a P-40, try to outmaneuver and perform acrobatics with a Jap Nate or Zero." He paused and grinned bleakly and sardonically, "Such tactics, take it from me, are strictly non-habit-forming!"

For psychological reasons this philosophy of combat was the hardest for Chennault to drum into his pilots' heads prior to combat. The precept to hit and run was contrary not only to the pilots' basically combative nature but to everything they had been taught in previous training. It smacked of running away from a fight. In fact, shortly after Chennault began to teach this theory, a British RAF group in Rangoon posted on its operations bulletin board a notice that any RAF pilot who was observed diving away from an aerial fight would be subject to court-martial. In the Chinese Air Force the penalty for the same "offense" was the firing squad. Chennault was not interested in vainglorious bravery or "loss of face." He could not afford to lose a single airplane or a single pilot and he was confident that the tactics which he was teaching in the teakwood classroom at Toungoo would not only give his men a victory ratio of four or five Japanese airplanes for every AVG fighter lost in combat, but would bring them back to fight another day.

This grim determination of Chennault's to insist upon his men doing what he knew to be right is a perfect example not only of his life-long independence and unorthodoxy; it demonstrated his iron will and his willingness and ability to do what he knew was necessary regardless of established custom or criticism. Time and time again, the soundness of his guerrilla air tactics was proved by the outstanding inequality in the battle results obtained by his AVG and the RAF and the U.S. Air Force. For example, in the battle for Rangoon, months later, the AVG and the RAF fought a united air battle against the Japanese. The RAF fighters hardly broke even with the Japanese in air victories; but the AVG chalked up the phenomenal victory ratio of 15 to 1. Much later, and in a different area of the war, 11 out of 12 U.S. Army Air Corps P-40s were shot down by a Japanese force of about 70 raiders over Fort Darwin, Australia, while 5 AVG pilots in the skies over Rangoon were shooting down 17 of a similar attacking enemy force without losing a single airplane.

It is another in the string of ironies in Chennault's career that this fighting force which the enemy could not down in combat almost met disaster because of spare parts shortages. Defeating the enemy in the air against staggering odds was a far less difficult problem than trying to win the desperate battle on the ground to acquire sufficient switches, radio tubes, oxygen bottles, carburetors, gun solanoids, batteries, and spark plugs. The principal need, a *sine qua non*, was airplane tires. Planes simply could not take off and land without tires. When all efforts to obtain tires had failed Chennault sent Joseph Alsop, the newspaper columnist who had joined the AVG as a staff officer as aide to Chennault, to Singapore on a desperate search for airplane tires.

Brooke-Popham had no tires but he did accept Joe Alsop's suggestion that he write a strong letter of recommendation to General MacArthur in the Philippines requesting tires for the AVG. The plan worked. The United States Navy provided PBY's to fly a consignment of tires to Singapore from which Brooke-Popham rushed them to Rangoon by boat. Months passed before other shortages almost critical were remedied but the arrival of the precious tires allowed the AVG P-40's to keep flying.

After two months of the hard Toungoo training routine which began at 6 a.m. with lectures, followed with flying exercises, winding up the day in organized athletics during the late afternoon, Colonel Chennault felt that his men were finally reaching a hard, sharp fighting edge. He divided his fewer than one hundred pilots into a group consisting of four squadrons and made his plans to send up pilots in pairs with one fighter protecting the other's tail. His plan was to use one squadron for initial attack, the second for support, with the third held as a clean-up reserve in the event additional planes were needed to finish a battle. This latter tactic he never put into practice because he never had sufficient fighter planes.

In the final days of training, the principal emphasis was on gunnery. Chennault knew well that no matter how skillful his pilots might be, they would be useless unless they could hit the enemy with their guns. Day after day he sent the AVG fighters aloft with only one instruction: "Dive and hit the target."

In October, Brooke-Popham and his aide, Air Vice Marshal Pulford, flew up from Singapore to inspect the AVG and were astonished at the progress Chennault had made in a couple of months. Always enthusiastic supporters of the AVG, these British officers furnished assistance without which Chennault was free to admit it would have been practically impossible to get the AVG into fighting trim. Equally helpful on the British side were Sir Archibald Clark-Kerr, then British Ambassador to China, and Sir Reginald Hugh Dorman-Smith, Governor of Burma, and his military commander, Lt. Gen. D. K. McCloud.

In October, the Monsoon season ended and on October 24, 1941, the first Flying Tiger patrols began over the airfields which the Japanese had constructed along the border of Thailand.

All intelligence reports pointed to mounting tension in Burma, and it became obvious that the Japanese were getting ready to strike hard toward the south in Asia. From mid-November onward Chennault and Tom Gentry, the AVG physician, began to spend the good bombing hours at dawn and dusk in the control tower at Toungoo, facing toward Thailand, looking for the Japanese bombers they knew would appear on the horizon one day.

It was December 8, 1941, on the far side of the International Dateline, when Chennault finished his morning watch in the field control tower at 11 a.m. and walked wearily across the airfield towards his quarters. Behind him he heard a shout and turned. Running was his radioman, waving a piece of yellow message paper. It bore the intercept of an American radio newspaper flash—the Japanese Air Force had attacked Pearl Harbor! Heavy Japanese bombers had caught the U.S. Air Corps, Army and Navy asleep early on Sunday morning and were raining bombs on airplanes parked on flight strips and on half of the United States Pacific Fleet, tied up at the docks.

The General briefing one of his fighter squadrons.

Joe dog—the General's mascot.

A group of Chinese pilots trained for the Chinese-American Composite Wing under the command of Gen. Chennault.

Part **3** *Time of the Harvest*

> *"The stone that was rejected by you, the builders, which has become the corner stone."*

ACTS 4:11

Chapter 13

Claire Lee Chennault stood on a small lecture podium of one end of the cement-floored, woven-bamboo briefing shack in Toungoo. Impassively, he waited for the pilots to find seats. War had come to the United States and suddenly the word had a new meaning for him. Terrible though the death and destruction had been during the past four long years, while China battled singlehandedly against the Japanese, the word "war" now meant something far bigger, far more important, far more personal.

As his eyes scanned that yellow radio message telling of the sudden sneak attack on Pearl Harbor, Chennault knew he was no longer fighting only for China. Now he was fighting for his beloved United States. Claire Chennault again became an American fighter pilot as completely as if he were once more wearing an Air Corps uniform. He began to speak to the AVG pilots in the briefing shack. He picked up the message paper bearing the fateful news.

"I've called you men together," said the AVG's Old Man calmly, "to tell you that the Japanese have attacked Pearl Harbor. That means our job will be much tougher than we had planned. It also means that we will no longer have to fight behind any kind of screen. We are the American Volunteer Group, and our job is no longer simply that of fighting for China. We are fighting for the United States now.

"We have the training to fight. We have the equipment. Now is the time we must turn to, and help
whip the common enemy. We won't wait until scheduled flight time this morning. I want patrols in the
air, and I want them up right after this meeting.
From now on, we stay on guard, on alert, 24 hours
every day. We don't intend to let any Japanese mission catch our fighters on the ground.

"That's all gentlemen. Thank you."

Chennault's main concern was that the Japanese
bombers might catch the AVG fighters on the ground
and destroy them. It was, of course, a foregone conclusion that Japanese air attacks would now be
levelled at the only remaining supply route into
China, the Burma Road. Guarding the famous road
was difficult for his tiny force since both ends had to
be protected at all costs: Kunming at the upper
terminus; Rangoon at the Burma end. Following the
surrender on October 8 of Thailand, the Japanese
had stocked a three-hundred mile network of Thailand air bases along the Burma border with fighter
and bomber planes. Additional bombers were based
at Hanoi, Indo-China, which the Japanese had occupied in 1940.

It was obvious to Chennault and to the British
in Rangoon that the lull before the storm would be
brief.

Lacking sufficient flyable fighter planes to create
the four squadrons he had originally planned, Chennault split his tiny force into three squadrons. The

first squadron, dubbed the Adams and Eves, was led by Robert Sandell of San Antonio, Texas. The second, called the Panda Bears, by John (Jack) New-kirk of Scarsdale, New York, and the third, Hell's Angels, by Arvid Olson, of Hollywood, California.

The British, on hearing the news of Pearl Harbor, had demanded that the entire AVG be transferred to Rangoon. After strenuous argument, Chennault finally retained direct command of Olson's Hell's Angels squad, which he transferred from Toungoo to Mingaladon Airport, ten miles outside of Rangoon, but he ceded operational control to the British. In other words, Chennault's fighters would be free to use the aerial combat tactics he had taught them but could be ordered into combat by the British air com-mander.

On December 18 the Japanese bombed Kunming and Chennault knew he would have to move his tiny forces to defend also the northern terminal of the Burma Road. He at once launched the first of the lightning-like moves which during the life of the Fly-ing Tigers in China made it impossible for the Japa-nese to catch them unaware and destroy them. Within an hour after Chennault's orders, they made the move to Kunming, refueling at Lashio. As the little force acted, the ever-careful, always-thinking AVG com-mander kept his first squad circling on patrol as the second squad made its takeoff from the Burma jungles. Upon arrival at Kunming the second squad patrolled while the first squad settled on the ground.

By the time dawn broke on December 19, 1941, an AVG fighter squadron was patrolling the air above Kunming and another was ready on the ground. Altogether, 34 P-40B's and their pilots were ready for the first Japanese move which Chennault knew was at hand. For more than four years he had been waiting and preparing for zero hour—the day when at his command American pilots in American planes would roar into the air to do battle against the Imperial Air Force of Japan.

He had only one regret at this juncture. He knew to his sorrow that the tiny fighter group which he now commanded was all of the men, planes, or equipment he would have for a long time. Hudson bombing planes which had been promised for a second American Volunteer Group, bomber pilots and crews and replacement fighter pilots, all enroute to China had instantly been diverted for use by the United States Army Air Corps as soon as the Japanese struck Pearl Harbor. Throughout the 19th of December, 1941, false alerts occurred but the long expected and eagerly awaited enemy planes did not appear. Then, at 9:45 a.m. on December 20, Chennault's special telephone linking him with the Chinese Code room, which in turn was tied in to the Yunnan Province air raid network, jangled clearly. Over the wire loud and clear came the voice of Colonel Wong Shu Ming, commander of the Chinese Fifth Air Force and the AVG's Chinese Chief of Staff. "Ten Japanese twin-engined bombers crossed Yunnan border at Laokay heading northwest. Their probable objective is Kunming."

"This is it," Chennault thought, and almost instantly his fast-working mind arrived at his battle decision. Against the oncoming bombers he would use twenty-four of his available thirty-four fighter planes. The first warning signal of an impending air attack, a single red ball three or four feet in diameter, was hoisted to the top of the warning mast at the Kunming airport. Pilots lounging in the wooden alert shack at the edge of the field, playing cards, reading and "shooting the breeze," peeled off jackets, sweat shirts and sweaters and quickly donned their heavy flying suits. They moved rapidly into the cold crisp winter air, headed for their planes and climbed into their cockpits adjusting their headphones, switching on their radios, making final adjustments to their parachutes. Then they waited.

The single ball was a warning that enemy or unknown aircraft had been seen or heard at a distance of about 180 miles. The alert was called the "jingbow," which was the American version of a word which sounded in Chinese like "jin-bao." It meant literally to be alert.

And now as the waiting pilots watched, a second ball went up on the airport warning mast. The enemy was getting close. A yellow flare flashed near the operation hut and twenty-four 1800-horsepower P-40 Alison engines coughed into life, backfired and shook the ground with their warm-up thunder.

Now a red flare meaning take-off. Almost at once the twenty-four fighter planes taxied in a group towards the end of the field looking like a school of sharks with wings, mouths gaping cruelly open, long white teeth shining. One by one, with wide-open throttles, they thundered down the strip and sailed into the air.

Chennault's battle plans, arrived at in a few brief moments between the first "jing-bow" and take off time, was simple. Four planes of the Panda Bears led by Jack Newkirk were sent to make the interception. At a point about sixty miles away four planes led by Jim Howard of St. Louis, son of former China missionaries, were dispatched to fly top cover, a defensive patrol at 22,000 feet over Kunming. Sixteen planes of the first squadron led by Robert Sandell of the Adams and Eves squadron, were directed to move to an auxiliary field just west of Kunming where they would stand by to join the battle at a decisive moment.

Chennault fired a red flare sending the second and first squadrons into the air and then drove with his executive officer, Harvey Greenwald and Col. P. Y. Shu, his interpreter, to a huge timbered clay pyramid on a slope overlooking the airfield. This was the combat-operations shelter containing duplicate sets of radio and phone communications with both the fighter planes and the warning net. Chennault, Greenwald and Col. Shu waited tense and silent in the field shelter checking reports from the Chinese net. In the skies overhead Jack Newkirk and his three mates, Bert

Christman of Fort Collins, Colorado, Ed Rector of Marshall, North Carolina, and John G. (Gil) Bright of Reading, Pennsylvania, tore through scattered clouds which rapidly thickened to heavy overcast as the planes roared to the southeast. Sixty miles from Kunming, Newkirk's little command spotted the bombers slipping in and out of the heavy cloud formations without fighter escort. Back at shelter headquarters the intercom radio system crackled with the excited voices of the four pilots.

"There they are, are they Japs?"

"No, no, they can't be."

"Look at those red balls on the wings!"

"Let's get 'em."

In the maddening silence that followed, Chennault waited. Then the radio exploded again.

"Shark Fin Blue calling base. Bandits sighted sixty miles east. Attacking."

In the air Newkirk signaled his wingmen and pulled the formation up high.

"Let's go!" Newkirk radioed and pushed his stick and throttle forward. Like slender deadly wasps the little formation of P-40's slanted down, air speed indicators climbing rapidly. With their engines wide open the fighters closed the gap and roared down and past the bombers, their 50-caliber guns in the nose and the four 30-calibers in the wings pouring a deadly hail into the bombers. Now the Jap gunners started shooting back and the Americans experienced the unfamiliar sound of lead pellets gutting into their ships.

Far below heavy explosions detonated as the Jap bombers jettisoned their bomb loads, dipped their noses for speed and swung frantically back toward Hanoi. Before the hard hitting P-40's could sail back up out of their power dives and reform, Newkirk's guns jammed and reluctantly he led his fighters back toward the base. One, however, Ed Rector, kept right on chasing the bombers. At this point Chennault's orders crackled over the radio to Bob Sandell's standby squadron. Behind this ten-plane combination came Robert L. Little of Spokane, Washington, with a four-plane reserve squadron. Jim Howard's formation continued the protective patrol over Kunming at 22,000 feet. The first AVG attacker to reach the Japs was Ed Rector who finally overtook the fast-moving bombers.

Rector dived steeply at the nine bombers, flying in three big V's. He kept shooting all the way in, which was why his guns stopped firing. He forgot the often-repeated Chennault admonition to fire in short bursts, but this was a very pardonable case of buck fever and despite this initial error in Chennault's "stay-alive" tactics, Ed got the bomber.

At the last moment, he saw parts of the bomber falling off as his bullets tore into it. He went under the bomber at such a close range he could see the rivets and the fine details of the plane's camouflage. He pulled out from the side and saw the tail gunner slumped over his gun with his jaw shot away—the reason he had stopped firing about half way in.

Rector watched the bomber very slowly fall out of formation, burning, and crash in a rice paddy. About this time Rector's gas gave out and Ed safely crash-landed in a rice paddy himself.

Now Bob Sandell's formation arrived with their guns and throttles wide open, followed closely by Bob Neale's quartet of planes. Bob Little and his three mates stayed high above as cover. At top speed, the heavy fighters tore down upon the lumbering bombers, their heavy 50-caliber guns riddling them at long range. Then, as the gap closed, the P-40's opened up with their their 30-caliber wing guns and the air became filled with crumpling bombers and P-40's trying to keep from colliding with each other.

The twin-engined bombers were moving at their maximum speed but could not escape the swift-flying fighters. A main gas tank on a Mitsubishi exploded with a roar and a great burning sheet of flame. The oldest AVG pilot, Louie Hoffman, 43, of San Diego, California, sent another Mitsubishi careening out of control. Fritz Wolfe from Shawano, Wisconsin, accounted for two bombers, smashing the gas tanks and engines of the first, and setting the second one on fire before it exploded.

Of the ten original bombers, only four were now in the air, and although all four managed to straggle across the Indo-Chinese border only one of them got back safely. It was an incredible first performance for Chennault's carefully trained but battle-inexperienced pupils.

Deeply satisfied, but quietly hiding his elation, Chennault called his pilots into the briefing shack, received their reports, and carefully mixed his compliments with a characteristic admonition.

"It was a good job, boys, but not good enough. Next time get them all."

The news of the victory created a sensation, not only in Kunming but throughout China and in every corner of the Allied world. That night the citizens of heavily bombed Kunming gave the AVG pilots a rousing, roaring celebration and throughout China newspapers gave the battle story banner headlines, calling the AVG fighters the *"Fei Hou"*—the Flying Tigers—a name that stuck with them forever afterwards.

It was a great moment in the long struggle of the Chinese against Japanese aggression. For years China's population had taken terrible beatings from the Japanese Air Force without being able to hit back. Not only the Chinese but the entire Allied cause in the Pacific took heart at this great air victory, following as it did a string of unbroken defeats.

Chennault was elated but not surprised. What had happened in the air was what he had watched happening so many times in his imagination. He was pleased that at last the air combat theories which he had advocated for more than twenty years and which the United States Air Corps had rejected had been dramatically proven. They were proven, also, to the complete satisfaction of the Japanese. Never again did the enemy attempt to send out bombers unescorted by fighter planes. In fact, they didn't return to Kunming at all for the next sixteen months and when they did they brought along a thirty-fighter escort.

The next ten weeks prior to the fall of Rangoon were among the AVG's finest. The odds were unbelievable. During the ten weeks, the AVG with never more than twenty planes that could fly, and sometimes as few as five, met the Imperial Japanese Air Force on thirty-one occasions and chalked up the incredible score of 217 confirmed victories and 43 probables. The cost? Four Flying Tiger pilots killed in the air and one while strafing. Another was taken prisoner. Sixteen P-40's were lost in combat. The RAF, fighting with the AVG during the same period, downed 74 Japanese airplanes, confirmed, with 33 probables. British losses were 22 Brewsters.

On March 1, 1942, following the fall of Rangoon, British Prime Minister Winston Churchill sent the following message to the Governor of Burma:

> The victories of these Americans over the rice paddies of Burma are comparable in character if not in scope with those won by the RAF over the hop fields of Kent in the Battle of Britain.

The senior British air officer in Burma, Air Vice Marshall D. F. Stevenson, noted that while RAF fighters in the battle of Britain faced odds of four to one, the odds against the combined British and American forces in South Burma ranged from four to one up to fourteen to one.

These were the days when the Japanese were hurling at Rangoon forces ranging from fifty or so bombers protected by squads of fighters, up to gigantic raids in which a total of 150 bombers and fighters took part. Day after day the American P-40's streaked through the skies, their guns blazing. Around sundown they landed in the dispersal airfields, bone weary, and covered with thick dust. But the men of the AVG seemed to thrive on tension and fatigue. Perhaps this was because they were able to relax in the evening. The wealthy British residents of dying Rangoon were filled with admiration for the colorful young American fighters whom they welcomed to their homes as guests. In the evenings the boys would have a few relaxing highballs with their British hosts as soon as they landed. After a hot bath, they dressed for dinner, often in tuxedos, and were ready for an evening on the town.

Usually after dropping their bombs, the Japanese would finish off their strikes by strafing the crowded streets of Rangoon, slaughtering hundreds of Burmese men, women and children. The wealthy British colonials began in increasing numbers to join the refugees leaving Rangoon. Many of them gave the keys of their magnificent homes to the AVG boys, saying "Enjoy it while you can but when you have to leave, burn it."

Chennault had tried to convince the British that

an early warning system was necessary, but the senior air officer who preceded Air Vice-Marshal Stevenson had believed that a single radar and one man at a telephone half-way between Rangoon and the Thailand border would be sufficient to furnish adequate warnings of Japanese bombers. As a result, often the first indication that Japanese raiders were on their way was a sudden "bombers overhead!" announcement from the Mingaladon public address system.

Time after time the dwindling force of P-40's rose to perform incredible feats in the skies against overwhelming odds. The planes were being flown so often that one after another went out of commision. But those that could be flown were flown—and magnificently. Typical of the spirit, skill, and heroism of the AVG pilots was their heroic performance on December 23 when 54 thundering Mitsubishi bombers protected by twelve Nakajima type-97 fighters and eight Zeroes roared in on Rangoon.

When the telephone rang in the alert tent, Squadron leader Arvid Olson listened, laid the phone down, and barked his orders: "Scramble. Japs on the way at 15,000. Get up to 18,000 and hit 'em out of the sun."

Twenty-one AVG pilots raced toward the 15 flyable P-40's standing ready loaded with ammunition and gas. Edward F. Overend, of Coronado, California, was riding away from the field on a bicycle for a day in Rangoon when he saw the rush of pilots to the field. Ed turned the bicycle, beat a running pilot to the nearest P-40, and climbed in wearing a white shirt and civilian trousers. Bob (Robert P.) Hedman of Webster, South Dakota, outraced another pilot to a P-40 and took off with the loser angrily waving a pistol at him.

Within five minutes, fifteen P-40's and eighteen British Brewsters were streaking into the bright blue sky. The American fighters split into two groups led by George McMillan of Winter Garden, Florida, and Parker Dupouy of Farmingdale, New York. They were waiting at 18,000 feet when the first wave of bombers thundered in. McMillan's planes shoved their noses down and dived, pulling up at the bombers' level to unleash a smashing assault from the side. The heavy 50-caliber guns on the P-40's shattered the bombers, sending metal and wood chips flying in all directions. Charlie Older of Los Angeles hit the bomb bay of the formation leader and the bomber exploded. George McMillan pumped a heavy load of lead into two bombers and both blew up.

Another AVG pilot, "Tadpole" (R. P.) Smith of Los Angeles, was one of the first two AVG pilots to become an ace—five planes knocked down in a single engagement. He did it with one of his guns firing out of control but he was able to swing his plane around so as to pour the runaway burst of fire into a second bomber, sending it hurtling down. Not satisfied, Tadpole unlimbered his 30-caliber guns and before he used up his ammunition he had shot down five enemy planes.

Bob Hedmein, known as a 'book flyer" during training days, also bagged five Japanese planes that day. Flying not by the book now but with a kind of inspired savagery and deadly precision he roared through a swarm of Nakajimas trying to guard a bomber, taking out one fighter plane on his way down, and then sending the bomber careening earthward. He pulled up and dived again, knocking out two more fighters on his second pass. Although his own plane was by now badly riddled, Hedmein overtook the disappearing V of Jap bombers, raced forward between the enemy planes and downed the flight leader.

The AVG casualties were Neale Martin and Hank Gilbert, killed, and the loss of Paul J. Green's P-40 which burned. Paul, a native of Clarendon, Texas, had not had time to don battle dress. When his plane began to burn he bailed out wearing only cowboy boots, shorts and a six-shooter revolver. As he dangled helplessly from his parachute harness, Japanese fighters circled, firing their machine guns at him. Green slipped his chute halfway down in an attempt to avoid the bullets and then appeared to have been hit. He hung limp the rest of the way down but when he landed, the ground crew came running up to find him untouched. He had been playing possum!

After this battle RAF air intelligence teams located thirty-two crashed Japanese airplanes in the rice paddies around Rangoon of which the British claimed only seven. The AVG had shot down a confirmed twenty-five enemy bombers and fighters, and had killed some ninety Japanese airmen with the loss of only two pilots and three airplanes! The RAF, bagging seven, suffered five pilot casualties and lost eleven fighter airplanes.

It was a great victory, but the Japanese now had moved a very large number of bombers and fighters into range and on Christmas sent over an enormous armada which now only twelve heavily-patched AVG P-40's and sixteen Brewster Buffaloes were left to face. Determined to knock out Rangoon, the Japanese used eighty-one Mitsubishi bombers protected by forty-two Nakajima fighters. The Japs had learned well the lesson which Claire Chennault had tried in vain to teach his own U. S. Air Corps for so many years: that even heavily armored and heavily armed bombers attacking without fighter escort cannot carry out their mission if enemy fighters receive adequate warning and are able to intercept.

But the Flying Tigers had also learned a valuable lesson during their great victory of December 23. Practicing the adapability and well-thought-out individuality which Chennault had emphasized during their training period, they adjusted their tactics. They had noticed that once the Nakajima fighter airplanes were separated from the Mitsubishi bombers they were trying to protect, they could not overtake the fast-moving bombers. Accordingly the new AVG tactics were directed at the earliest possible separation of fighters from bombers during Japanese raids.

It was during this Christmas attack that the Japanese tried a trick that very nearly worked. As two of the Tigers were diving into a group of Japanese fighters, over their radioes came the clear order: "Pancake immediately"—a signal to land. The two pilots began to let down when mechanics on the ground waved them frantically away from the strip. The Americans, gunning their engines, climbed back into the sky away from the six Nakajimas that were diving on them. The AVG had just undergone a first case of English-speaking Japanese pilots issuing fake orders in English.

During the Christmas battle in the skies over Rangoon, which lasted almost an hour and a half, another of Chennault's lectures about the ruggedness of the P-40's and the relative fragility of the Japanese Zeroes paid off. At 18,000 feet Parker DuPuoy's planes ran into a twenty-seven-plane group of Japanese bombers and their Zero escorts. Diving through the Zeroes with wide-open throttles, Parker and Freddy (Fred. S.) Hodges of Memphis, Tennessee, each smashed a Zero and dived on the bombers. Bill (William N.) Reed of Marion, Ohio, shot a bomber's tail gunner just before a British Buffalo fighter zoomed in to finish off the Jap. It was at this time that DuPuoy, with Chennault's oft-repeated lectures engraved deeply in his brain, deliberately crashed his wing into a Zero as the Jap tried to turn away. Down sailed the Zero's wing, snapped off at the roots. Parker DuPuoy looked around and found four feet of his

P-40's wing had been sheared away and an aileron smashed. For more than half an hour he wrestled with the crippled controls, finally landing his plane at high speed without sustaining a scratch.

After landing, with almost empty gas tanks, the P-40 pilots were jubilant. The squadron leader, Arvid Olson, radioed Claire Chennault in the Kunming headquarters: "We got fifteen bombers and nine fighters. Could put entire Jap force out of commission with whole group here."

The official count for Christmas Day credited the AVG with twenty-one of the twenty-eight Japanese bombers and fighters shot down. Eight additional bombers, never counted officially, dropped into the Gulf of Martaban. Again, the British were credited with seven victories. The AVG lost two P-40's and no pilots; the RAF lost nine airplanes and six pilots.

Again, throughout China and the Allied world flashed the amazing news that a tiny American volunteer air force deep in the Asian jungles was winning the only battles of the war against Japan, and winning them against incredible odds. It was a tale straight from a fiction writer's typewriter but it was true. Overnight, the Flying Tigers of Chennault had chalked up the air victories, unequalled in the annals of air warfare, which would make them famous around the world for decades to come.

In Kunming, my husband felt not only a warm glow of pride for the success and heroism of his men, but a deep satisfaction that his once unorthodox theories of air combat had now been so fully proved and vindicated that never again could they be challenged. Not for another two years would the U. S. Air Corps admit that Chennault had been right for more than twenty years and send out fighter escorts with its ETO bombing squadrons over Nazi Germany, following enormous casualties. But closer to the scene of the AVG triumphs, in the Pacific Theater most of the air fighters, principally in the Navy swung completely over to the Chennault brand of air combat tactics. Renewed life and hope surged through war-weary China and Claire Chennault could now feel quietly confident that his Air Force, miniature though it might be, could nevertheless survive despite the most powerful blows of Japan's mighty Air Force, while dealing punishing, often crippling, blows in return.

Their Christmas Day thrashing convinced the Japanese that it would be very unwise to risk another Flying Tiger clawing until they could bring overwhelming force to bear. For the next several weeks they switched to night bombing in defense of which the Rangoon RAF pilots carried the load, while the AVG led daytime strafing attacks on Jap airfields inside Thailand. These were successful. A large number of Nakajimas and Zeroes were put out of commission as they rested on the ground.

AVG personnel not on active fighting duty were performing the equally important task of combing the Rangoon docks for usable lend-lease supplies.

Lend-lease had begun flowing following the President's authorization in the Summer of 1941. Anything remotely usable was packed on trucks and sent on the long and hazardous journey to China via the Burma Road.

By late January, the Japanese were ready to have another go at knocking out Rangoon. So thoroughly had they learned Chennault's lesson that bombers must be escorted by fighters, that on January 23 when the big Japanese air fleets began pounding Rangoon, they were employing three-to-one fighter plane protection for the Mitsubishi bombers, and within five days they were sending nothing but Nakajimas and Zero fighters.

The rapidly shrinking American and British Air Forces downed fifty Japanese bombers and fighters with the loss of only two AVG pilots during the heavy, sustained assaults between January 23 and 28. Not even the heroic round-the-clock work of ground crews could keep restoring the badly mauled P-40's forever. The rugged P-40's took combat punishment which no other airplane then in manufacture could have sustained, but by the end of January there were only ten of them left in Rangoon. Chennault relieved the hard pressed "Hell's Angels" squadron by moving in Bob Sandell and his first squadron "Adams and Eves."

It was a glorious but costly period for the AVG. All of the six AVG flight leaders saw heavy combat action in the skies above Rangoon and the

Martarban Gulf. Olson, Sandell and Newkirk were killed. Sandell died testing a repaired P-40. Jack Newkirk was gunned down as he dived on a Japanese armored car. All of them, including the remaining three, Tex Hill, Bob Neale and Jim Howard, accounted for heavy Japanese casualties and maintained a flaming spirit in the AVG that refused to be dampened by heat, green mold, overwork, or Japanese fighter planes. At the end of the heavy late January raids Jack Newkirk had radioed Chennault at Kunming: "The more hardships, work and fighting the men have to do, the higher our morale goes. Squadron spirit really strong now."

In mid-February, 1942, the fall of Singapore released additional Japanese air units and the enemy now began to hit Rangoon with up to two hundred airplanes daily. It became clear that Rangoon could not hold out much longer. Bob Neale's AVG squad was down to nine P-40's when the Japanese, on February 25, began their final assault on Rangoon. As an overture they hurled one hundred sixty-six airplanes against the pathetic total of fifteen fighters which the combined AVG-RAF could muster. The AVG knocked twenty-four enemy planes out of the hot skies over Burma but on the next day the Japanese were back with an overwhelming force of two hundred bombers and fighters. The six still flyable P-40's bagged twenty-four enemy aircraft without the loss of a single plane or pilot. Nevertheless, when the bone-weary pilots landed their battle scarred P-40's, it was clear to squadron leader Bob Neale that the end had very nearly been reached. The tires of the remaining fighter planes were badly chewed. Battery plates were so thin they would not function for more than a single day with a recharge. In all of Rangoon there was no Prestone oil coolant left.

Fresh food was gone; water for drinking difficult to obtain. The heavy clouds of dust generated by the high temperatures on the airfield clogged the P-40's Allison engines so badly that sometimes they would not start. The civic authorities of Rangoon, unable any longer to furnish living facilities or food for their prisons, insane asylums, and leper colonies, had released the wretched inmates of these institutions. Block square areas of Rangoon were burning. Before the American pilots could stock up on precious oxygen or recharge their plane batteries, the British acting under final scorched-earth orders, destroyed every remaining battery charging and oxygen storage unit. When Bob Neale learned that on the night of February 27 the British had removed the one remaining radar spotting unit, he knew that the end had been reached. He dispatched four of the P-40's still able to fly, with a tail-end AVG truck convoy up the Burma Road and along with Tadpole Smith began the final evacuation of Mingaladon Airfield.

Rangoon fell.

Chapter 14

After the fall of Rangoon, the P-40's that were still flyable and the British moved to Magwe, about two hundred fifty miles north of Rangoon on the Irrawaddy River.

For the sadly depleted Flying Tigers, facing Japanese Air Forces of between four hundred and five hundred airplanes based in southern Burma and Thailand, the war now became an offensive hit-and-run affair in which the AVG fighters struck whenever they could catch the enemy on the ground and moved from field to field to prevent Japanese strikes from catching them parked and vulnerable. Two long-cherished Chennault concepts now came into play to save the day. One, now that the AVG was on and all-out hit-and-run, guerrilla operation, put pilots under orders to come to earth on a different field from their take-off point. Another old Chennault trick also worked well: building fake P-40's loaded with hay so they would burn convincingly and staking them out where they could be spotted and bombed by the enemy. Often, AVG pilots lay under well-camouflaged airplanes watching Japanese Mitsubishi bombers waste high explosive bombs and incendiaries on a nearby field filled with make-believe airplanes. On such evenings an hour or so later the Flying Tigers would laugh as old "Tokyo Joe" and other

Japanese broadcasters announced in triumphant tones that the invincible Japanese Air Forces had destroyed an entire group of AVG fighters.

It was very fortunate that despite a far-flung spy net work in Burma and China the Japanese never learned or could accept the true statistics concerning the minute numbers of combined AVG-RAF forces arrayed against them. Often, to the intense amusement of the British and American sky battlers, Tokyo broadcasters spoke of the "thousands of planes used by the American guerrillas." Obviously, this erroneous belief worked to the tremendous advantage of the AVG in the heartbreaking days when combined American-British air strength fighting a strictly rear guard action in northern Burma totalled less than thirty fighter planes and a dozen elderly Blenheim bombers. Japanese pilots were instructed to avoid head-on air battles with the AVG and to attack American P-40's only when they were refueling, parked on airfields, or in repair shops. Chennault's masterful guerrilla strategy insured that this was seldom.

During this critical period of the war, my husband's chronic bronchitis flared, making him so ill that on many occasions he was unable to travel. When things grew serious, despite a burning fever and wracking coughs, the AVG's chief surgeon, Tom Gentry, could not keep Chennault in bed. The AVG commander's rickety old Beechcraft transport plane might as well have been a hospital plane, for despite his illness,

Chennault was apt to appear at any time at the critical points of the theater. His old Beechcraft was so worn out that pilot Johnny Hennessey, of Boston, could not call upon it for any unusual strain for fear its engines would quit. It was a strictly stop-and-go aircraft which Johnny was forced to land at odd points—on roads, plowed up fields and even hillsides. Fighter pilots with tongue only halfway in cheek often said they would prefer meeting Japanese fighters in the skies than flying in the Beechcraft. When the "Old Man" of the AVG was too ill to fly at all, he kept in touch with every base by radio, although at times his voice grew so hoarse that he practically needed an interpreter.

It is important to realize that the AVG was never defeated in Burma. It was the powerful Japanese ground forces, not the air forces, that were responsible for the steady retreat northward of the AVG and the British, plus the Burmese, Indian and Chinese ground forces. Only when Japanese ground forces overran air bases did the AVG move—never before.

Magwe was difficult to defend as the victorious Japanese ground forces steam rollered northward in Burma. The lone radar which the British had brought from Mingaladon was pointed south, but there was no warning net west of Magwe. A single British Blenheim bomber flying at 10,000 feet about eighty miles to the east afforded the only spotter for incoming Japanese raiders from Thailand. On top of the difficult conditions, the Japanese opened their all-out raid on Magwe shortly after noon on March 21. In the ensuing twenty-four hours the Japanese sent a total of two hundred sixty-six bombers and fighters roaring in to crush the Americans and the British. A heavy wave of fifty-four Mitsubishi and twenty Zeroes roared in in the first wave, burned one P-40 and wiped out six or seven Hurricanes and all of the Blenheims on the field. Four of the Allied fighters took to the air and knocked down four of the raiders but the effect of the massive Japanese onslaught was crushing. From Kunming, commander Chennault, listening to the Magwe raid from his hospital bed, radioed a warning to his men to watch for a follow-up raid. The raid arrived simultaneously with his telegram. In addition, the complete breakdown in radar enabled the Japs to sneak in without warning and they were able to inflict greater damage than any other Japanese assault upon the AVG during the entire war. Not a single AVG or British fighter gained the air and when the unmolested Japanese bombers finished their work of devastation, Zeroes zoomed in and expended their ammunition unchallenged. The terrible attack left only three flyable P-40's on the field and out of twenty-five British Hurricanes only four were still able to fly.

In Kunming over the violent protests of Chief Surgeon Gentry, Chennault arose from his sick bed at Kunming University Hospital. With Bob Neale and other flight leaders he made a retaliatory mission. The total force of P-40's Chennault could assemble for the mission numbered six fighters from the first squadron and four from Jack Newkirk's second squadron. The ten fighters took off from Kunming early on March 23, refueled at Loi-Wing and at dusk landed quietly on two airfields near the Thailand border. At four a. m. on the twenty-fourth they took off and roared down upon Chiengmai Airfield where they found more than forty Japanese bombers and fighters warming up for a raid. The Japanese planes were loaded with bombs and high octane gasoline and as the P-40 tracers knifed into the enemy planes they exploded in a roar of flame. Not one plane was able to leave the ground. Pilots and ground crews were strafed as they scurried for shelter. The fields were a flaming Hell when the P-40's roared away. It was on this occasion that Newkirk was killed by the return fire of the Japanese armored car. Another loss was William D. ("Black Mack") McGarry, of Los Angeles, whose plane was shot down in the teak forests of Thailand. McGarry, unhurt, was arrested by local police and placed in a Bangkok jail for the remainder of the war.

Despite the loss of two great pilots, the Chiengmai raid was an air victory for the AVG and the British. Burma's Air Vice-Marshal Stevenson radioed, "Many thanks for the breathing spell furnished us by your magnificent attack at Chiengmai." Later it was learned that Bob Neale's attack had wiped out an entire Japanese air regiment, the survivors of which were returned to Japan to be fitted into new flying squadrons.

In the spring of 1942 good news came to the Flying Tigers. Brand-new, improved model P-40E's (Kittyhawks) packing six .50-caliber machine guns in the nose and wings, with droppable belly tanks, bomb racks and higher speed, had been purchased by the Chinese Government in the U. S. and were enroute to the AVG in China. Ten AVG pilots were sent to ferry in the new fighters from the docks of Takoradi on the Gold Coast of Africa. Some time later, the twenty brand-new fighters arrived in Kunming.

But by mid-April total AVG strength, including the new P-40E's, was down to 251 men, including all ground and staff personnel. Thirty-six airplanes were fit to take to the air and thirty-nine P-40's were under repair, although there were no spare parts. Up to now, forty-one fighter planes had been lost in combat and crack ups. Additional P-40E's would arrive in Takoradi in June, but not until the fall of 1942 would a mere third of these reach China.

Loi-Wing enjoyed an especially good air raid warning protective net. This was fortunate because these were days when the northern Burma war in the air was reduced to sneak hit-and-run attacks by Chennault's tiny forces and when the extreme mobility which he had dinned into his personnel paid dividends. Time and again, Mitsubishis and Zeroes dived on airfields they believed and hoped were filled with American planes and personnel, and found nothing.

Day after day, AVG forces, usually only two airplanes and occasionally made up of groups of four to six, hit the Japs unexpectedly, smashing their personnel, planes and barracks.

As April 29, the date of the Emperor's birthday drew near, Chennault remembered another Emperor's birthday in 1938 when his expert planning had enabled Russian pilots to annihilate Japanese attackers. He reasoned that the Japanese, believing him to be ready for them, would try something different. He decided it was quite likely they would stage something for the 28th so that on the 29th, the day of the Celestial Emperor's birth, they could announce a great victory.

On the morning of April 28, an AVG dawn patrol over Burma noticed great activity along the entire Japanese front, and Chennault ordered every flyable P-40 into the air. Instructions were to land at a subsidiary field, Mongshih, instead of Loi-Wing, at the end of the day. He instructed five of his fifteen fighters, a force commanded by Tex Hill, to fly cover at upwards of 15,000 feet; ten more led by Arvid Olson would fly in two layers at 10,000 and 12,000 feet respectively. On that morning the Japanese sent over twenty-seven Mitsubishi bombers with a large escort of Zero fighters flying behind and above them heading for Loi-Wing. Simultaneously, they hit Lashio on the Burma Road itself, with a mixed group of bombers and fighters.

The AVG pilots spotted the first group of bombers

halfway between Lashio and Mandalay. The American force divided, half slamming into the oncoming escorting Zeroes, the other half heading for Lashio. When it was all over the total results were twenty-two Zeroes downed with no AVG losses.

But despite the AVG victories in the air, the Japanese ground on through the jungle and that afternoon reached Lashio and the Road. This made the Loi-Wing base too dangerous to occupy longer and with sickness in their hearts the AVG set fire to twenty-two P-40's being repaired in the Loi-Wing workshops and retreated out of Burma to new bases at Paoshan and Yunnanyi in Yunnan Province, China. Like a juggernaut, the great masses of Japanese ground troops were pushing the allied front northward through the Burma jungles. And on May 1, the day after the AVG evacuated, the first Jap ground troops arrived in Loi-Wing.

Actually, the AVG personnel were not sorry to leave Loi-Wing. It was dangerous fighting an air war in the jungle and the most successful of air efforts cannot succeed for long if the protecting ground troops are unable to hold the air bases. The Flying Tigers were worn from combat fatigue, lack of sleep, and the continuous effort to keep old and bullet-splattered equipment functioning. By the end of April, all had been in sustained combat for five months.

Four pilots had died in battle. They were Neale Martin, Hank Gilbert, Bert Christman and Louis

Down at the line with the men who keep 'em flying, Maj. Gen. Chennault talks over mechanical details of one of the fighter planes that rolled up a ten-to-one victory score over the Japanese. He is talking to Sgt. Walter J. Zarowski of Newark, N. J. Working on the far side of the engine is S/Sgt. Fay Palmer of Vanwert, Ohio, while S/Sgt. Floyd E. Anderson of Boise, Idaho, bends over his job. Brig. Gen. Edgar E. Glenn, Chief of Staff, stands beside Gen. Chennault.

Lt. Gen. William Hood Simpson, Commanding General Ninth Army, is greeted at the Kunming airfield by Maj. Gen. Chennault while Maj. Gen. Henry D. Aurand, Commanding General Services of Supply, looks on.

Maj. Gen. Chennault at his desk, Headquarters, Kunming, China.

("Cokey") Hoffman. Two men—Tommy Cole of Clayton, Missouri, and Jack Newkirk—had died in low-level strafing raids on the Japanese. Bombing raids had killed two: Frank Swartz of Dunmore, Pennsylvania, and Crew Chief John Fauth. Nine others had died in accidents of one kind or another.

In spite of their losses and their deep fatigue the AVG pilots were still performing magnificently, superbly trained for their work and stimulated by the great challenge they faced. Considering the formidable opposition, their losses were small. But on the ground, and in operational flights which lacked the stimulating qualities of air combat, their weariness began to make them careless. Landing accidents increased.

The medical staff was almost as weary as the pilots. A quartet of doctors headed by Chief Surgeon Tom Gentry, and including Joseph S. Lee of San Francisco, Samuel B. Prevo of Whiteland, Indiana, and Lewis J. Edwards of Coffeeville, Kansas, assisted by two nurses, Jo Buckner Stewart of Dallas, Texas, and Emma J. Foster of Pennsylvania, were almost as weary as the pilots. On many occasions and during the last days of Rangoon they worked long and desperate hours bringing aid to the civilian bombing and fire victims as well as to their own AVG personnel.

Chapter 15

On April 28, after the fall of Lashio, General Joseph ("Vinegar Joe") Stilwell began his historic retreat out of Burma into India and the Jap advance moved northward at a faster pace, heading up the Burma Road in new captured British trucks with the obvious intention of crossing the Salween and Mekong Rivers and taking Kunming.

On May 3 the Japanese reached the tiny border-town of Wanting in Yunnan, and the threat to Kunming became grave indeed. The only obstacles in the path of the Japanese on the road to Kunming consisted of a blown-up bridge across the Salween River and Chennault's Flying Tigers.

A few miles directly east of Wanting, the Salween River crosses the China-Burma border in a mile-deep gorge which flood waters have carved in the solid rock during the passing centuries. The Burma Road winding northeast into China crawls along the crest of the Salween River gorge and for twenty miles or more skirts sheer precipices as it coils down the mountain in a series of hairpin turns to reach a suspension bridge across the Salween.

In early May, the victorious Japanese ground forces, now well established in Lashio, and occupying Wanting and Kutki, began clearing the way to the river on their confident march toward the key to the entire Chinese military jigsaw—Kunming. To the keenly analytical military mind of Claire Chennault, it seemed obvious that if Kunming fell, China would be virtually out of the war. For without Kunming the Chinese ground forces of Chiang Kai-shek would have no supply gate to the outside world and the Japanese, in turn, would have won a strategic base from which to launch further penetrations into India and the remaining areas of China. Chennault at once determined to do everything in his power to halt the Japanese although knowing full well that his tiny force of fighter planes might prove no match for the numerous and heavily armed Japanese ground forces. Carefully, he reviewed the situation.

Across the Salween River from the advancing Japanese, Chennault had divided his American Volunteer Group into three sections. The headquarters base was at Kunming. At Paoshan five P-40's were stationed to protect AVG truck convoys coming up from Burma, and halfway between Paoshan and Kunming a radio and servicing detachment at Yunnanyi served as a refueling depot.

Paoshan was attacked on May 4 without warning by fifty Japanese bombers and its refugee-packed streets became a bloody charnel house for thousands of Burmese and Chinese refugees fleeing northward before the advancing Japanese. A lone AVG pilot, Charlie Bond, from Dallas, Texas, got his P-40 off the ground and downed two bombers, but Ben C. Foshee of Red Level, Alabama, was struck and killed by bomb fragments as he ran toward his plane.

On the next day Chennault struck back with nine

P-40's which intercepted a follow-up attacking force of Japanese bombers and sent eight of them crashing to earth.

Meanwhile, returning P-40 reconnaissance planes brought news of the inexorable advance of the crack Japanese Red Dragon armored division which was spearheading the enemy's northward drive. With it moved well-armed infantry units in trucks, with artillery, automatic weapons, cannons, and large stocks of ammunition, gasoline and bombs. This powerful force before which British, Burmese, Indian, and Chinese opposition had melted away, was now approaching the west bank of the Salween River. The retreating Chinese had wrecked the suspension bridge, but Japanese engineers with pontoons were observed nearing the river. Chennault knew that if the Japanese got across the Salween there was nothing to stop them from driving on to the strategic prize, Kunming. He also knew that if he were to order his planes to attack the Japanese columns winding down the cliffs toward the river hundreds of the Chinese and army refugees who were filling the twenty-mile-long corridor down the mountainside would die.

On May 6, Chennault radioed to Madame Chiang Kai-shek in Chungking for instructions, personally outlining the military situation and the difficult choice that must be made. Within an hour, he had the answer.

Generalissimo instructs you send all available AVG to attack trucks, boats, etc. between Salween and

Lungling City. Tell AVG I appreciate their loyalty and redoubled efforts particularly at this critical juncture . . .

Knowing Madame Chiang Kai-shek and the Generalissimo as he did, Chennault knew, too, the pain they surely felt at sending him the order that would entail the killing of innocent Chinese. But he also knew that not to do so would endanger all of China and he applauded the difficult decision. That evening he held a blackboard council of war with his pilots. The AVG armorers, Roy Hoffman of Athens, Ohio, and Charlie Baisden of Scranton, Pennsylvania, rigged bomb racks for 570-pound bombs under the bellies of four "Kitty Hawk" P-40E's and loaded the wing racks with fragmentation bombs. For weeks Chennault had been pleading with Washington for light bombers with which he would be able to attack the mechanized Japanese columns driving up from Burma but the improvised bomb racks on the P-40E's was the best he could do at the moment. Previous experiments to mount makeshift racks for the old P-40B's had not been successful.

Leading the four-plane formation of Kittyhawks with their bombs was Tex Hill and with him were Tom Jones, Ed Rector, and Frank Lawlor, all former Navy dive-bomber pilots. Others who volunteered for the Salween gorge bombing mission included Lou Bishop, Lind (C.H.) Laughlin, Jr., of Ashland, Missouri, Frank Schiel of Prescott, Arizona, and Bob Little.

Assigned to fly cover in P-40B's, high above the improvised bombing squad, were the leader, Arvid S. Olson, with Tadpole Smith, Erik Shilling, a trio of ex-Army pilots, and Tom Hayward formerly in the Marine Corps.

At dawn on the 7th of May, the tiny eight-plane force composed of four new fighter planes with home-made bomb racks and four nearly worn-out fighters took bravely to the air to try to halt the crack divisions of the victorious Japanese Imperial Army.

The Flying Tigers encountered bad weather over Paoshan. The Monsoon season, which had already enveloped Southern Burma, was moving north and facing the P-40's were towering thunderheads. But there was no turning back. The eight P-40's plunged into the dark, turbulent storm area and after fifteen minutes of very rough flying, broke suddenly into clear skies.

The sight that met the eyes of the eager Tiger pilots was almost too good to be true. Ahead, and etched against the towering rock cliffs of the steep, twenty-mile winding descent to the muddy Salween at the bottom of the knifelike gorge, was the entire Japanese military force. Japanese engineers were working frantically to unload pontoons out of trucks and into the river. Miraculously, there was no sign of Japanese air support. Evidently the Japanese high command believed that the American Volunteer Group had been pounded out of existence.

Tex Hill waggled his plane's wings and down

roared the quartet of fighters-turned-bombers in a diving attack on the rear of the slow-moving columns trapped against the rocky mountainside. Mixed in with the Japanese soldiery were the innocent, non-combatants—and this was the great pity of the thing. In accordance with the pre-battle plan as discussed with Chennault, the Kittyhawks loosed their big demolition bombs at the top of the Salween gorge with devastating effect. Huge boulders, landslides of rubble, trucks, ammunition and human bodies exploded in a shattering blast that piled up into a bloody barricade barring any possible retreat for the Japanese.

Pulling out of their dive, the Kittyhawks climbed steeply, dipped their needle-like noses, and came screaming in again, this time with all of their fifty-caliber machine guns spewing deadly lead. Simultaneously, they unleashed the fragmentation bombs under the Kittyhawks' wings which tore great holes in the truck and infantry columns, already faltering to a halt because of the sudden incredible attack which had literally come out of the blue.

Back and forth along the narrow mountainside road like deadly darning needles, the P-40's weaved, pouring death from twenty-four fifty-caliber guns into the confused and helpless Japanese. After the Kittyhawks had exhausted bombs and bullets, Arvid Olson and his three wingmates came tearing in to strafe the trapped Japanese vehicles and personnel again.

Unscathed by ground fire, all eight P-40's streaked to Yunnanyi where they were quickly rearmed with fragmentation bombs and incendiaries. The second strike was led by Jim Howard, whose squadron destroyed more trucks and automatic weapons and machine-gunned the fleeing tank crews, scuttling vainly for cover. A huge, irregular coil of black acrid smoke rose slowly over the decimated Japanese column.

Encouraged by the tremendously successful aerial onslaught of the Americans, the Chinese forces dug into their mountain fox holes on the west bank of the Salween, emerged to attack the Japanese with courage, if not with efficient weapons. They had nothing heavier than rifles and hand grenades. At the same time, from the east bank, Chinese forces which had been routed by the Japanese, paused in an about-face and poured an effective machine gun fire into the disorganized and demoralized Japanese columns across the river.

For the next three days, Chennault hurled his fighters against the helpless Japanese in the Salween gorge. With new heart, the Chinese recrossed the Salween and savagely attacked the Japanese flanks as the enemy force recoiled up the road and back toward Burma. Out of the huge force trapped in the Salween gorge only a fraction of the once-invincible Red Dragon Armored Division was able to fight its way out and fall back to Lungling.

The Japanese drive, which, had it been successful, might have won the day for them in China had been halted, blunted and turned back by a force of eight men in eight airplanes. Riding in on the moment of AVG triumph, the Chinese ground forces armed with a new and flaming spirit blocked the next weak attempt of the Japanese to cross the Salween which did not occur until June. The Japanese attempt failed and with the arrival of the heavy Monsoon rains the big Japanese drive into southwest China was smashed.

Chennault kept up the air pressure on the Japanese supply lines, effectively stalemating the enemy which, although entrenched on the west side of the Salween for two years, was never able to advance farther. In the summer of 1944, Chinese ground forces supported by the U. S. Fourteenth Air Force crossed the Salween from the north and began the slow but steady offensive that eventually forced the Japanese back into Burma.

In my opinion, which is shared by qualified military experts, few feats in modern warfare compare in drama with the success which Claire Chennault had in the battle of the Salween gorge. It was a modern Thermopylae. With eight planes and inspired timing, strategy, and tactics, my husband had won one of the greatest victories of World War II. With four new, and four very old, airplanes he had successfully accomplished a mission which the combined British, Burmese, Indian and Chinese armies had not been able to achieve. Chennault, with eight planes, had done what General Stilwell with all of his ground forces had not been able to do. He had stopped the Japanese war machine.

Chapter 16

Tom Corcoran, the General's close friend has often remarked that Claire Lee Chennault was a lucky man. By so saying, he never meant to imply that it was luck, rather than genius, that enabled Chennault to accomplish what he did. Rather, it has always seemed to Tom Corcoran that in the entire life of Claire Chennault, from the little dreaming boy on the Tensas River in Louisiana, to the very end of his long career, Chennault was able to succeed magnificently not only because he had the heritage, the early upbringing, and the natural mental and physical qualities with which he was born, but also because he happened to come along during the period that saw the birth of the airplane, the trial period for aviation during World War I, and afterward. As Tom Corcoran often remarked, "He was on the corner when the parade went by!"

What Mr. Corcoran meant was that in addition to the accidents of birth, place of birth and chronological time of birth, Claire Chennault matured to early manhood during a time in which nothing much had been proven in regard to the airplane or its tactical military use. Thus, with his original and inspired ideas, he was actually—despite the formidable and intrenched inertia and opposition which he encountered—able finally to have his theories accepted.

Again, in order to do this, he needed a series of—for him—fortuitous situations which might easily be termed "lucky" in retrospect. Thus, if his health had not failed in 1936, he might have been less than receptive to the offers coming from China. After his arrival in China, had the Japanese not decided shortly thereafter to make their bid for domination, he might not have been able to observe the Japanese in action and form his theories of air tactical combat which later saved the lives of his AVG pilots and spelled ruination for the Japanese Imperial Air Force.

The list is long. His health, which had previously failed in the United States, could well have failed again in the stifling, insect-plagued Burmese jungles or the hot humid summers or cold damp winters of China. In the numerous air battles in which he emerged not only victorious but unscathed, he might have been killed. One might even go so far as to imagine that had his own country's high brass been more understanding of the true conditions prevailing in China and the necessity to bring to bear powerful American air forces, the need for exercising the infinite resource and the imaginative evasive tactics which kept his tiny air force alive might never have existed.

On any one of a number of occasions, the Japanese might have been able to wipe out his command. The old, rickety Beechcraft in which he flew so many miles during the war in China, might have crashed. The unfortunate opposition from his own countrymen, such as General Clayton Bissell, might have been sufficiently vitiating to have nullified his best efforts. Finally, in Tom Corcoran's own words, "The situation in China was exactly what Chennault needed in order to function to the maximum extent of his potentialities. In the close-packed organization of a highly organized existing air force in the United States or even in a European theater, his genius might never have had a chance to flower. But in the desperate, loosely organized, improvised and personal kind of war that was going on in China, his imaginative spirit had full fling. All his innate genius and all of the magnificent technical training he had had in his years in the United States Air Force expanded in the Chinese conditions like a coiled spring. In the United States he was too light to buck the line but in China he was a brilliant open-field runner and quarterback. Here he could be Hannibal; here he could be Stonewall Jackson.

"It was no accident that after he had shown what opportunities there were in China for imaginative men of his own stripe, there was a constant effort of like-minded men to join him in circumstances in which they too could function as they wanted to function—as fighting men, rather than as organizers of 'flying desks' in Washington. It is significant that in the Air Force of today, in which there is a constant demand upon men to meet technological conditions that are changing faster than at any time in military history, many of the foremost men of vision in today's

U. S. Air Force are graduates of the 14th Air Force, who learned and profited from their service with Chennault in China."

During the weeks following the victory in the Salween gorge, Claire Chennault needed all of his genius. The AVG had staved off China's collapse, but the outlook was still far from bright. China was now cut off from all land communications with the Allies except for the ancient Silk Road across the Turkistan Desert to Russia. But because of Russia's struggle for survival at Stalingrad, this road was useless. The only other avenue over which supplies could reach China was over the highest mountains in the world, the route over the snow-capped, soaring peaks of the mighty Himalayas known as "The Hump." Of all the problems that Claire Chennault faced in the desperate days of China, supply was, and would continue to remain, his most critical problem.

The collapse of Allied resistance in Burma had enormous effect on the pattern of the war in southeast Asia. Gone was the Allied dream of supplying Chinese armies with modern British and/or American equipment and then throwing the great weight of China's unlimited manpower against the Japanese. The gateway to China was now closed to everything except air power, and the tonnages required were enormous.

Another effect of the Burma debacle was Vinegar Joe Stilwell's burning desire to wipe out the sting of his defeat in Burma. In early June, Stilwell presented an extraordinary proposition to Generalissimo Chiang Kai-shek. He proposed that all Chinese army units be reorganized with American officers holding all posts of Colonel and higher rank. This plan, firmly rejected by the Generalissimo, nevertheless remained Stilwell's objective and was one of the major reasons for the final parting of the ways between the two men.

Within weeks after Pearl Harbor, on December 30, 1941, the induction of the American Volunteer Group into the U. S. Army had been authorized, but nothing much had been done about it until March 29, 1942, when Chennault was called to Chungking for a conference with Generalissimo and Madame Chiang, General Stilwell, and Colonel Clayton Bissell, who had been sent to CBI to handle the China end of the Jimmy Doolittle Tokyo raid. Bissell had remained as Stilwell's air officer.

There was no love lost between Bissell and Chennault, but that was little reason for Bissell's failure to inform Chennault of the nature of his mission. As a result, when Doolittle's raiders, forced to change their plans, arrived over China in darkness and bad weather, Chennault's vast warning net, spreading over east China, had no way of communicating with the American bomber pilots to guide them over the unfamiliar terrain. Of this, my husband wrote in his private papers:

If I had been notified, a single AVG command ground radio station plugged into the east China net could have talked most of the raiders into a friendly field. As it was, they all crashed or bailed out in the dark. Doolittle himself bailed out near the Japanese lines and narrowly escaped capture. One crew flew past several friendly bases to crash in Japanese-held Poiang Lake where they were taken prisoners. Three of these crewmen were eventually executed at Shanghai. My bitterness over that bit of bungling has not eased with the passing years.

With the Generalissimo's support, Chennault strongly opposed the induction of the American Volunteer Group. Its record had never been equalled by a regular Army or Navy group of comparable size. Chennault felt it would be criminally wasteful to sacrifice the group's spirit and experience in exchange for a change in uniform. He felt that the AVG was unique, especially trained for a special task which it has performed with phenomenal success. Its combat record had proved the soundness of Chennault's theories to the satisfaction of all except some of his Air Corps fellow officers and he felt that absorption of the AVG into the Air Corps ranks would blunt its fine fighting edge and destroy much of its effectiveness.

The Army's reasons for demanding induction was that the paperwork required to supply a non-regulation organization was too difficult to justify or maintain. Bissell and Stilwell made it quite clear during the March 29 conference that the AVG would be denied further supplies if it refused induction. Chen-

nault was unwilling to withdraw from the war for
any reasons and agreed at once to accept a return to
active duty but made it clear that his men would
have to make their own decisions.

Chennault believed, logically, that his long experience in China, combined with the AVG's incom-
parable combat record entitled him to primary
consideration for the post of Commander of the new
Air Force unit in China. Washington disagreed. On
February 13, 1942, Laughlin Currie sent the following radiogram:

> Arnold (General 'Hap,' commanding the Army Air
> forces) is of opinion you are A-1 combat man and has
> fullest praise for AVG but wants member his own
> staff to head larger show stop (Millard F.) Harmon
> not available while (Lawrence) Hickey not a staff
> man leaving only Bissell stop Harmon says Bissell
> now changed to your views on tactics stop Bissell can
> pull more stuff from army this being essential for
> larger efforts stop We feel proposed setup deserves
> fair trial because China's interest demand good
> tactics as well as good material support stop We
> hope you will cooperate and participate stop Your
> promotion to Brigadier General will shortly be made
> stop.

Chennault, feeling that General Arnold would
never allow a military "maverick" like himself to
receive an important command, had suggested Major
General "Miff" Harmon and Colonel Larry Hickey
as possible alternatives and because he could not for-

get Bissell's laughable tactical school theory about the only successful way in which fighter planes could attack bombing planes. Bissell quite seriously had advanced the incredible theory that fighter planes should drop a long ball and chain device in order to foul the propellers of enemy bombing planes.

Chennault's orders to active duty arrived on April 9, promoting him from his retirement rank of Captain to temporary Colonel. Nine days later, he was promoted to temporary Brigadier General. Although he was senior to Bissell in the regular Army, Bissell's promotion to Brigadier General was dated one day earlier than Chennault's. This made him senior to Chennault—an old and effective Army maneuver.

During the negotiations in Chungking, Stilwell and Bissell seemed to Chennault to be concerned mainly with the early dissolution of the AVG, without advancing any clear thoughts on how they would obtain replacements or fight the air war in China without it. They insistently advocated April 30 as AVG discharge date, but Chennault countered with July 4 as "dissolve day" feeling that by that date a replacement group could and would be furnished. Madame Chiang Kai-shek supported him on the July 4 date and it was so agreed.

It was inevitable that the AVG would be less than enthusiastic about rejoining the services. All were reservists and most had joined the volunteer group as an escape from the very discipline and discrimination by regulars which they knew a return to the service would force them back into. Furthermore, they were war weary and dissillusioned with the failure of the United States Government to supply the spare parts they so sorely needed, which they blamed on red tape and inertia. They did not wish again to become a part of the mechanism responsible for the delays in supplying the oxygen bottles, tires and carburetors for the lack of which they had seen comrades crash and die. To Chennault their bitterness was understandable.

When Bissell asked Chennault to make a personal appeal to the group to forego a much-needed furlough he refused, bluntly telling Bissell that the AVG had served a year on foreign service and seven months of combat under the worst of conditions. Bissell knew by now that the Army would not be able to provide replacements to meet the July 4 deadline and asked permission to make a speech to the AVG at Kunming. Chennault agreed and assembled the group in the auditorium of Yunnan University shortly after the battle of Salween gorge. He warned Bissell that the men might not receive his proposal with warmth but Bissell, having the weight of authority on his side, was confident. He gave them all of the reasons why he thought they should stay on in China and then gave them his punch line: "And for any of you who don't joint the Army, I can guarantee to have your draft boards waiting for you when you step down a gang plank onto United States soil."

The reaction of the AVG to Bissell and especially

to his tactless speech with its implied threats was predictable. With his swagger and spit-and-polish, he represented all they had been glad to leave behind when they volunteered for action in China. Most of the boys refused to join the Army. Many preferred to go home but remained from affection for Claire Chennault, loyalty to the outfit, and belief in the cause.

At midnight on July 4, 1942, the American Volunteer Group passed into history. This group, which military experts had predicted would not last three weeks in combat, had fought valorously and successfully for seven months over most of Burma, China, Thailand and French Indo-China. It had destroyed 299 Jap airplanes with another 153 probably destroyed, with a loss of only twelve P-40's in air combat and sixty-one on the ground, including the twenty-two which were deliberately burned in a "scorched earth" move in Loi-Wing. Four AVG pilots had died in air combat; six had been killed by anti-aircraft fire and three by enemy bombs on the ground. Three had fallen prisoner to the enemy and ten more had died in flying accidents. The group had defeated the Japanese air force in more than fifty air battles without a single American defeat. Its great record had won most of its members decorations from the Chinese Government, and British and American Distinguished Flying Crosses had been bestowed on ten pilots.

Chapter 17

The China Air Task Force (CATF) replacing the AVG—a hard outfit to follow—had a short life, and not a very merry one. Its life span covered, however, an extremely important period in the history of World War II in China. It was a period which saw some of the best of the AVG warriors choose not to remain in China as members of the U.S. Armed Forces, preferring to return to the United States.

Many of the decisions of these men were influenced by the fear of renewed regimentation and the feeling that to "join up" would be knuckling under to the threats of General Bissell whose "invitation" to the AVG members had sounded to them more like a "join or else" threat.

The General, in his personal papers, said of the China Air Task Force: "It was patched together in the middle of combat from whatever was available in China during the gloomy summer of 1942. That was precious little. CATF, the stepchild of the 10th Army Air Force in faraway Delhi, had to fight, scream and scrape for every man, airplane, spark plug and gallon of gasoline."

General Stilwell had promised Generalissimo Chiang Kai-shek to replace the AVG with a full-strength Air Force fighter group of four squadrons and a hundred planes. On the change-over date agreed to by them, July 4, 1942, Generalissimo Chiang Kai-shek found that he had exchanged the veteran AVG for three newly activated squadrons of the 23rd Fighter Group—a group that existed largely on paper. In cold actuality, the army supplied only a dozen green pilots and twenty clerks and mechanics. Everything else in the newly organized 23rd Group consisted of AVG equipment which had been bought and paid for by the Chinese. From the United States Army came no fighter planes, no trucks, no jeeps, no radios, no administrative or maintenance equipment —not even regulation uniforms. In fact, Army ground equipment for the 23rd Group did not reach India until a year later in the summer of 1943. It did not reach China until the next fall.

Claire Chennault preferred always to fight in the open for what he unhesitatingly believed to be right. However, faced with devious maneuvering, he "fought fire with fire" and resorted to a certain type of subterfuge. As he records in his memoirs:

The Fourth squadron for the group was acquired by subterfuge. The 16th Fighter Squadron of the Tenth Air Force, 51st Fighter Group was bogged down in the Monsoon weather of India's Assam Valley where fighter operations were impossible during the summer. By inviting a single flight at a time to China for 'experience' I lured the entire squadron to Peishiyi during June and July and never returned them.

The 16th was well equipped with Kittyhawks (P-40E) and veteran pilots. After the departure of the

AVG's these experienced pilots of the 16th—Johnny Alison, Ed Goss, Johnny Lombard, Harry Pike, Harry Young, and George Hazlett—furnished most of the CATF combat leaders. The 16th stayed on in China until the end of the war and fought through all the hottest actions along with the 74th, 75th and 76th squadrons of the 23rd Group.

Even the Japanese knew more about the true facts of the transition of AVG to CATF than did the American people. To cover up its strange dealings, the War Department slapped a heavy blanket of censorship over the transition. The excuse, of course, was the often-abused ground of military security. Nightly, the Japanese radio blared accurate details of the transfer. The War Department, however, never stopped pretending that all had gone well with the AVG induction. As late as January 1945, the War Department informed the House Military Affairs Committee of Congress that 220 of 250 AVG personnel had been inducted into the Army in China on July 4, 1942. This in the face of official War Department records which still show that five staff officers, five pilots and nineteen ground crew men accepted induction on that date.

Nevertheless, from this miserable beginning, the CATF—the only American Air Force fighter group activated in the middle of combat—the 23rd Fighter Group went on to become the backbone of the American Air Forces in China and one of the greatest fighter groups in the world. Along with the 5th Air

Force's 49th Fighter Group, the 23rd shared the honor of being the longest group in continuous combat against the Japanese. During the three years of its history, the 23rd destroyed 941 enemy aircraft and maintained an air combat superiority of better than five to one.

During the summer of 1942 the total offensive fighter plane force available for the 23rd group were fifty-one war-weary veterans of the AVG—thirty-one Tomahawks (P-40B's) and twenty Kittyhawks (P-40E's). Of these only twenty-nine were flyable. At Stateside training fields all of these planes would have been hauled off to a salvage heap. In China they were expected to defeat the Japanese in the air. Not until the closing days of 1943 did the last P-40B of AVG vintage reach the Kunming salvage depot. This was more than two and a half years after the AVG had been assembled in Rangoon.

Despite General Hap Arnold's often-repeated statement that only new planes were being sent to Army Air Force combat units, the replacement planes for China—when they finally reached there—were P-40K's that had already flown hundreds of hours in training schools and combat. Some, sent to China from North Africa, had swastikas painted on their cockpits testifying to their previous combat service against the German Luftwaffe. A year later, when the first North American Mustangs (P-51's) reached China, they had already undergone from 100 to 150 hours of training school battering in Stateside centers before Chennault's pilots received them for combat.

The Japanese, on the other hand, were coming out with at least one new fighter-type plane every year and generally managed to send two or three improved models against the Americans during each fighting season in the East China campaign. Nevertheless, until the fall of 1944 the main American combat work in the air was done with P-40's.

General Chennault considered the P-40 a fair medium-altitude day fighter and an excellent low-flying ground strafing plane. But because Chennault had nothing else, his men used the P-40 for everything that an air force must do. Among the American pilots it was a joke that "if we only had a periscope we could use the P-40 as a submarine."

Although it had not been designed for night work, Chennault at times used the P-40 as a night fighter and a night bomber. It was the P-40, dive bombing with belly tanks loaded with rifle ammunition, rice and pork meat that brought the Chinese their first relief when their western armies ran low on food and ammunition. When a mechanic or staff officer had urgent business at outlying points throughout China, he wormed his way into the baggage hole of a P-40 and rode in constricted blackness to his destination.

A single P-40 plane with a borrowed RAF camera which had seen AVG service did all of the CATF's photo reconnaissance. The P-40 was, perhaps, the greatest all-purpose work-horse combat plane in history. When the newer P-51B's finally arrived in the fall of 1944, Chennault's men were not sorry to see the old P-40's finally go. But to the Chinese, the shark-nosed P-40 plane would always be the symbol of their deliverance from the terror and horror of unrestricted Japanese bombing and of the sorely needed help that the American flyers gave to China in her hour of sorest need.

The short but active life of the China Air Task Force constitutes a record as incredible as that of its predecessor, the AVG. With a top fighting strength of forty fighter planes and seven bombers, the CATF confronted a Japanese Air Force totalling 350 to 450 planes spread over a 2,000-mile arc from Hankow through Hong Kong and Indo-China to Burma. Chennault's only defense was, as usual, good offense. The only hope for survival was in guerrilla tactics— using mobility and supplies to strike the Japanese all along their perimeter in a desperate attempt to prevent them from concentrating their forces for a knock-out blow against China and the bases of the CATF.

During the early weeks of the CATF, a number of AVG veterans stayed on out of sheer loyalty and devotion. Of them—and of all the CATF—my husband spoke in terms of highest praise, often by name.

I remember his telling me of Colonel Robert Lee Scott, Jr. Bob, a West Pointer, had come to China as a transport pilot. He became enamored of the life of a fighter pilot, and stayed on to fight valorously in the P-40's. He was another in the large group of southerners who always seemed especially attracted toward flying and the Flying Tiger type of flying in particular.

Bob Scott soon endeared himself to Chennault and to men by his selflessness and disregard of rank. He was a "bird" colonel who had been commander of the 78th Pursuit Squadron in Panama and had begun his Far Eastern career by ferrying supplies in DC-3's. After he joined Chennault, he insisted on demoting himself to a wing man in order to learn the Flying Tiger techniques. He went along on every strafing or bombing mission he could and after Bob Neale left on July 19, Bob Scott became commander of the 23rd Group.

Not all of the Army pilots to reach China came close to Colonel Scott in training or ability. Many paid for the inferior quality of the instruction they had received with their lives. They had little air gunnery practice, no navigating experience and a smattering of formation flying. Most had never flown a P-40. Five among the early arrivals confessed they were afraid to fly combat and were sent back to the Air Transport Command.

One group to arrive had been called from the 51st Group in India—the poorest of the bomber and transport pilots. These men were sent to China to be fighter pilots. Colonel Scott asked his group if there were any with more than 300 hours flying time. Not a single hand was raised and the entire group was sent back to India that same afternoon. Green pilots were a tremendous liability. Chennault had neither the time, the gas, nor the planes to spend on training them in China. If they were sent into combat immediately, they jeopardized the lives of the veteran pilots by inability to hold formation and lack of flying ability.

However, a number of exceptional pilots reached China in 1942. Many of these were developed from a group of bright young West Pointers whom Clayton Bissell, a fanatic for meticulous staff work and detailed reports, had sent to China to bring Chennault's command a bit more of the West Point type of orderliness and spit and polish. But instead of doing this, they accepted the AVG combat tradition and became fighter pilots.

Among the best were Colonel Clinton B. (Casey) Vincent of Natchez, Mississippi, who had been sent to China to be Chennault's chief of staff. To season him, Chennault sent him into some of the hottest battles over East China during which he shot down six enemy planes. He learned fast and well and a year later, at the age of twenty-nine, he became the youngest general in the Army Air Force and the second youngest in the United States Army. He commanded the East China Task Force.

Another officer, Colonel Bruce Holloway, selected by Clayton Bissell to be the CATF operations officer, likewise became an expert fighter pilot. In a few weeks the slim, slow-speaking Tennessean had learned just about all that General Chennault could teach him. During the year, Bruce Holloway ran up a score of thirteen Japanese planes shot down and wore himself to a frazzle. Chennault sent him home for a rest despite his violent protests. Later, he commanded the first jet-propelled group in the AAF.

General Chennault was a natural leader. One factor in the incredibly high morale of his men under extremely adverse conditions was the appreciation he poured on them for good performance. This is exemplified by his comments to a foreign correspondent on the heroic performance of his men, including his great ace, Bob Neale, in the hectic days of the air-battle for Rangoon:

"On Wednesday (February 25, 1942), three of my boys shot down four Japanese pursuits in ten minutes during one battle, and forced twenty-three others to run. The boys just charged into the Japanese formation and broke it up.

"In another battle on the same day a handful of AVG planes, outnumbered almost ten to one, routed a formation of forty Japanese planes. Within thirty minutes, eighteen Japanese fighters and one bomber were definitely shot down. Seven more were probably shot down. The Japanese then ran.

"You should have seen Bob Neale. He didn't sleep for two days and two nights, but he kept going somehow. What a guy! He's a wild man in the air, that guy. His plane was an awful mess. He landed it with both tires flat and never even cracked it up. The windshield and instrument panel were all shot up, and there were seventeen bullet holes in the tail. I don't see how he got down."

Bob Neale had the greatest number of confirmed kills of all of Chennault's brilliant fighter pilots.

Among the many colorful men associated with Chennault in China was Merian C. Cooper whom Chennault described as: "A character from the Hollywood movies he once directed." Colonel Cooper had been a combat pilot in World War I. He had also organized the Polish Kosciuszko squadron to help Poland fight against the Russian Red Army in 1920. Cooper was the only American besides George Washington and Abraham Lincoln to have a life-size statue of him erected in Warsaw.

On an intelligence mission to Russia by way of China, Cooper was stalled in Chungking waiting for a Russian visa that, because of the long Soviet memory, never came. One day, Cooper appeared at Peishiyi, carrying his bed roll. He announced that he was tired of sitting around in Stilwell's Chungking theater headquarters and wanted a job with a group that was fighting. He stayed on, proved himself a brilliant tactician and a prodigious worker, assisting Chennault in engineering some of the most successful CATF forays. He used to ride in the nose of the lead bomber peering over the bombardier's shoulder, during strikes he had previously planned.

Cooper, no diplomat, made little attempt to hide his contempt for the Stilwell-Bissell policy of weak defense in India and neglect of the excellent strategic possibilities of striking closer to the Japanese homeland by intelligent use of air power in China. Bissell began urging Cooper's return to the U.S. on grounds of ill health, and finally persuaded Stilwell to issue the necessary orders to send him back to Washington. There Colonel Cooper continued to tell the true story of the Stilwell-Chennault situation to anybody who would listen. He knew that by doing so he was sacrificing all chance for promotion. Later, General George Kenney recommended Cooper many times for a general's star, but it seemed that the War Department's memory was as long as the Russian's! Colonel Cooper had committed the unpardonable crime of being frank and truthful about a situation Stilwell and his superior officers were trying to becloud with censorship.

Another outstanding member of the fine group of World War II flying aces Chennault was fortunate enough to have with him at this time was Johnny Alison. Major John R. Alison, of Micanopy, Florida, had originally been sent to England in the spring of 1941 to train British pilots in the P-40. Later he was assigned to Russia to train Russian pilots. Finally he obtained clearance for combat duty and arrived in Kunming by way of India.

Johnny Alison, a slightly built young man, had courage and determination. One of the many victories won by Chennault's Flying Tigers was engineered and brilliantly carried out by Alison. In doing so, however, he very nearly lost his life.

When Alison arrived in Hengyang, assigned to the 75th Fighter Squadron as deputy to the commanding officer, Major David L. ("Tex") Hill, there appeared to be nothing happening. But the lull was short-lived. On the second night after Johnny's arrival, the far-flung Chinese warning net reported heavy engine noise heading toward Hengyang. Johnny Alison and the other fighter pilots went outside the hostel to watch. For ten, fifteen, eighteen minutes they heard and saw nothing, but the warning net was always most accurate and they waited expectantly. There was the chance that the bombers might not be heading for Hengyang, but the odds were that Hengyang was the target for tonight.

Finally, they heard the bombers coming—a deep drone that grew to a roar as the heavy bombers passed overhead in the dark night sky. The Americans had not made a steady practice of trying to knock out night bombers. The P-40 was not a night fighter and the precious planes were well hidden and camouflaged. When the Japanese did attack by night they usually managed to plaster only the dummy P-40's staked out on dummy airfields near the real airfields.

As Johnny Alison watched the bombers move overhead dropping their eggs of death, he could clearly see fire jetting out from the engine exhausts. The exciting idea of rising to meet the bombers and being able to locate them by the visible exhaust flashes came to him and he made known his idea to the others, "Tex" Hill, Captain Albert T. ("Ajax")

Baumler, and others. Baumler, an experienced fighter pilot who had fought in the Spanish Civil War also thought night interception was feasible.

Since the P-40's were not equipped for night fighting, elaborate preparations were necessary. Alison and Baumler and several other pilots gave considerable thought to the problem and the plans they would use when and if the Japanese bombers came over again. A night or two passed without the din of a tin can being beaten with a stick by a coolie—the usual announcement of an impending night air raid. Nevertheless, the boys were ready and on the third night the coolie beating the tin can roused them from their mosquito netting-draped bunks. Dressing as they ran, the pilots raced for their P-40's.

They climbed into the dark cockpits, turned on the switches for battery and generator, and peered at the gauges, levers and switches. They were hard to read by the dim cockpit lights designed for emergency use. One by one, the long in-line Allison engines coughed and came alive with a roar that could be heard ten miles. One by one, the dark green fighters with the grinning red and white teeth of the shark's mouth painted behind the air scoop raced down the runway. At about 100 miles an hour the planes began to bounce and the pilots pulled back on their sticks, sending the straining fighters zooming into the dark night sky. They climbed steadily at about 150 miles an hour, circling to their left by prearrangement, as they rose to meet the bombers that the field

Lt. Col. John (Pappy) Herbst, Commanding Officer of the 74th Fighter Squadron and leader of Leapfrog operations.

Celebrating the 1st anniversary of the 14th Air Force. Left to right: Lu Han, commander Yunnan troops; Lung Yan, governor of Yunnan; Gen. Chennault; Dr. H. H. Kung, Minister of Finance; Jerry Huang, director of War Area Service Corps.

Crew members of four transport planes of the 14th Air Force. The officers and men successfully carried out a hazardous night mission to Hengyang, ancient Chinese city where a besieged Chinese garrison had held out more than a month against repeated Japanese assaults. Sixth from left in the rear row is the transport section's commanding officer, Lt. Col. John H. Williamson of Ninety Six, South Carolina.

radio told them were still heading straight towards Hengyang.

Up they climbed—9,000 feet, 10,000 feet, and at 12,000 feet Alison levelled off. It was too dark to spot Ajax Baumler or the others and he began to circle, straining to see through the darkness. Suddenly the radio began to emit strange beeping noises, garbling the voice of the operator in the radio shack on the ground. The last words he heard were: "Three twin-engined bandits coming in from north to south. . . ." then a break, and ". . . looks like they are making a turn to come back." The Japanese jamming closed in and he could hear no more. Suddenly, he spotted the bombers. Small bluish-white lights were streaking from the exhaust pipes.

Alison and Baumler closed on the enemy immediately. Alison was nearest and attacked the first wave of three enemy bombers, flying in V-formation. As he brought the left-flying bomber squarely in his gunsight, he saw flashes of light to his right as the bomber flying to the right and rear of the lead bomber opened fire. Alison's P-40 was hit repeatedly as the Jap's shells crashed through fuselage, cockpit, and engine. Alison simultaneously pressed his gun trigger, releasing all of his six .50-caliber guns, each loaded with 300 rounds of mixed tracer and armor-piercing bullets. It was a desperate gamble now. Could the P-40, with shells from the bomber on the right thudding through it, cripple the bomber in his sight ring before it—or Alison—was fatally hit.

The P-40 with its heavier fire power won. The bomber ahead streamed oil and black smoke and suddenly veered off wildly to the left, out of formation. Ajax Baumler, coming in behind Alison, kept the falling bomber in his gun sight and finished him off.

Alison immediately banked his faltering fighter to the right and attacked the bomber that had been firing upon him. After a few bursts from his battery of heavy fifties, which were returned, the bomber veered crazily off-course as a wing tank blew up in a great blast of yellow fire.

The third bomber, leading the V, had continued steadily on its course, and was now dropping bombs. Alison knew his time was running out. His cockpit and controls were shot up and smoke was beginning to trail from his knocking engine. Nevertheless, Johnny went after the third bomber. He rapidly overhauled it in his faster P-40, and again pressed the trigger. These were crucial seconds, as he carefully aimed his guns. His engine was now bucking and the entire plane was vibrating from the stricken engine. With his last few rounds of ammunition, Alison saw pieces fly off the lead bomber, then a bright orange flash. The bomber rolled completely out of control and plunged down, streaming fire. Several crew members managed to bail out, but some died anyhow, for their parachutes were on fire.

Now Johnny Alison's problem was to stay alive. He was approaching a dark field in a stricken airplane, but knowing the importance of preserving any aircraft capable of being landed, he began his last desperate gamble of a desperate evening. He would ride the dying fighter in. The engine was now smoking and burning and as he reached 3,000 feet or so the engine suddenly went dead. In an eerie silence Alison grimly fought the partially jammed controls, trying to bring the P-40 in at the required landing speed of at least 100 miles an hour. To do this, he had to dive steeply and pull out just in time to make a deadstick landing. Difficult enough in daylight, this was almost impossible over a darkened field at night.

He almost made it. At the last moment, by the light of the moon he knew he would never be able to land on this run and through sheer instinct, although the engine had died minutes before, he pulled back on the stick and thrust the throttle forward.

Oddly, the engine coughed, seemed to catch—then spewed flame. It looked for a second or so that he would have enough momentum to carry him over the trees lining the field near the river. But the engine died again and there was no momentum left to come around for another try for a field landing. Johnny did not want to cross the river and smash into thickly populated Hengyang. There was only one thing to do and he did it. Narrowly missing a bridge, he pancaked down into the dark cold river, struggled out of the cockpit and, burdened by heavy clothing, began to swim toward the shore. He was semi-conscious, for upon impact he had cracked his forehead on his instrument panel and his face was streaming blood.

The Siang River was about 200 feet wide at the point where Alison ditched. Dimly, he could see a raft tied to the town side of the river and desperately he began to swim toward it, dimly outlined in the light of the moon. Heavily weighted down with clothing, he found it tough going in his somewhat shocked and dazed condition.

A young Chinese boy came out and helped pull Johnny onto the raft and then from the raft to the river bank. Here, three Chinese soldiers were waiting with their bayonets pointed at him. They did not, of course, know in the dark, whether he was an American or a Japanese survivor from the air battle that all had witnessed.

Alison pulled out a small Chinese flag, waved it, and spoke the few Chinese words he knew, saying that he was a "Mei-gwo-Ren" an American. Finally the Chinese soldiers were satisfied that he was not a Japanese and took him to a small house where he rested while the tension flowed out of him. He made his way, early the next morning, back across the river and on to the flying field.

Meanwhile, Tex Hill, another great flying ace of World War II, enraged by what he thought was the death of Johnny Alison, had roared into the skies with his team mates, as another Japanese attack came. This wave of enemy planes—forty Zero fighters— was apparently seeking revenge for the destruction of four of the six Japanese bombers the preceding evening. Never daunted by great odds, ten P-40's led by Tex, had risen to plow into the forty attacking Zeros.

At this point there occurred one of the first Kamikaze dive bombing attacks of World War II. Tex Hill, enraged and blazing with raw courage, had just finished heading his P-40 straight for an enemy Zero. On collision course the two planes roared toward each other and Tex Hill was the one that did not budge.

The Japanese plane gave ground and began to trail smoke. He went into a spiral above the town. Apparently the pilot, mortified by his failure to meet Tex Hill head on and still alive and knowing his plane was doomed, had deliberately headed his Zero straight down for the American airfield in a screaming, smoke-trailing dive. Ironically, when he crashed with a great explosion into what he thought was a group of American planes, all he had succeeded in doing was killing himself and destroying some of the fake P-40's staked out on the dummy airfield.

The final sequel to the story of Johnny Alison's narrow escape from death occurred twenty years later, in the United States, long after the end of World War II, when Johnny Alison was introduced to a fellow member of his company, the Northrop Corporation, a Ph.D. named Tsien. "We've met!" said Dr. Tsien. He was the same Chinese boy who many years before had pulled the bleeding, shocked

American pilot out of the Siang River after his amazing night's work in the dark skies over Hengyang. Of this, Johnny Alison said recently:

"It is still incredible when I think that out of 600 million or more Chinese this one random individual who gave me a hand in the backwoods of China is today a doctor of philosophy and a top engineer in the company for which I work."

I have previously recounted the flaming spirit of Colonel Ed Rector who refused to break off an attack on Japanese bombers, even when the bombers had turned tail and were scuttling for safety. This never-give-up spirit was typical of Ed Rector and his career was one of the brightest of all of Chennault's brilliant young pilots.

The numerical odds which the CATF faced were staggering. With a top fighting strength of forty fighters and seven bombers, the CATF faced a Japanese Air Force totalling 350 to 450 planes dotted along a 2,000-mile arc from Hankow through Hong Kong and Indo-China to Burma. Its only defense was a good offense. The only hope for survival lay in employing mobility and surprise—striking the Japanese all along their perimeter to prevent them from concentrating their forces against the CATF for a knockout blow.

The CATF's best fighter pilots were in the 75th Squadron under "Tex" Hill, the 76th commanded by Ed Rector, and the 16th. These squadrons, along with the Mitchells of the 11th Bomb Squadron, were or-

ganized into an extremely mobile air task-force capable of striking anywhere in China within forty-eight
hours. Even General Chennault's headquarters was
organized to fit into a DC-3, continue operations in
flight, and be ready for action within an hour after
landing.

But vital though organization and mobility were,
the single most important ingredient was the caliber
of the men doing the fighting. The same spirit that
sent "Tex" Hill up to avenge the supposed death of
Johnny Alison, kept "Tex" on with the China Air
Task Force when, like most of the other AVG fighters, he could have left for other better paying em-
ployment. "Tex", a former Navy torpedo and dive
bomber pilot had no love for the Army. He stayed
with General Chennault merely "because somebody
has to finish this dirty job" and during the critical
days of the China Air Task Force he wore himself
to a frazzle.

Throughout most of the summer of 1942, "Tex"
flew with acute malaria. But the enemy would never
have believed they were facing a sick man. During the Japanese air blitz against Hengyang, "Tex"
flew to Hankow alone at night to dive-bomb the airdrome. Hankow was then the most heavily defended
Japanese base in China, and "Tex's" one-man air
raid kept the Japs too busy to bomb Hengyang that
night.

Of "Tex" Hill, my husband once told me,
"It was his type of leadership that kept a strong AVG

flavor in the CATF and 14th Air Force and made so many pilots and ground crews in China continue to work and fight so hard when everything else went wrong and all other motives lost force and meaning."

Another great fighter pilot was Johnny Hampshire, whose brief career was comet-like in its brilliance, and sudden ext inguishment. Johnny Alison, in a recent letter to me, told the saga of Johnny Hampshire:

"There are a number of stories concerning events and personalities in the China Air Task Force and Fourteenth Air Force which have human interest value but for one reason or another have received little publicity.

"While I was in China, a young fellow from Grant's Pass, Oregon, was perhaps the top pilot and potentially the greatest ace of the war. There is no question but that he intended to be the war's greatest ace. Unfortunately, this kind of determination makes one an easy target for fate and his career ended early, but not before his determination had written a brilliant but brief chapter in the history of aerial warfare.

"His name was John Hampshire and he reported to my squadron in the Fall of 1942, after General Chennault had made a special plea to General Arnold to send reinforcements who were experienced. John was with a group of experienced P-40 pilots who had been flying patrol in the Caribbean out of Panama. They were all good and contributed materially to the strength of the young Fourteenth Air Force. John was an attractive boy, always laughing, with a competitive spirit which made him want to win at everything.

"When each new pilot reported to duty with my squadron I personally took them up and tested their skill in formation flying, formation acrobatics and individual combat, although individual combat with the Japanese was highly unprofitable and forbidden by Chennault because of the superior maneuverability of the Zero. Simulated dog fighting between two P-40's gave me a good appraisal of the other pilot's skill. When I first flew with Hampshire his capability in formation was exceptional. Although it was relatively easy for me to best most of my pilots in individual combat because of my senior experience, not so with young Captain Hampshire. On our first try it was all I could do to keep from being resoundingly defeated. I held my own on my honor but I recognized that here was a pilot of unusual skill.

"When we landed I congratulated him and then turned to his crew chief who had met us at the airplane. When I asked him what had been the condition of Captain Hampshire's fuel tanks prior to takeoff, Hampshire broke into loud laughter. The crew chief admitted that he had been forbidden to completely fuel the airplane on the orders of the captain. Although in these contests I had a rule that the aircraft would be completely fueled, as the weight of the fuel made a considerable difference in the performance of the aircraft, I joined in the laughter. It was obvious that this presumptuous newcomer to the squadron had tried to pull a fast one on me. But I admired, and was pleased to have as a member of the squadron, an officer with an overwhelming desire to win. I was sure this would come in handy in our contest with the Japanese, and it certainly did.

"In addition to being an expert pilot, Hampshire was a rare combination of pilot and gunner. On two clearly defined occasions there were Japanese on my tail, shooting, and I was a pleased witness to Hampshire's marksmanship as I watched them explode. Seeing a Zero explode was always an exhilarating sight, but it is not hard to explain the pleasure that results from witnessing one explode when you are full of fear that he is about to shoot you down.

"Another example of Hampshire's excellent marksmanship occurred one day over Lingling. At this time I had turned command of the squadron over to Major Ed Goss and he recounted this incident to me. The Japanese brought a reconnaissance bomber across the airfield at about ten thousand feet heavily escorted by fighters. Over the field the bomber opened its bomb bay doors and released a shower of leaflets challenging us to a fair fight.

"I wish I had saved one of these leaflets as it was worded in a stilted Japanese manner stating something to the effect that they admired us for coming so far from our home to fight in this hopeless struggle; that they recognized that the Imperial Japanese

Fighter Command was the greatest in the world and therefore they challenged us to a fair fight.

"These words were no sooner out of the bomber's bomb bay when it exploded in the midst of its fighter escort and the pieces came tumbling to the ground around our air base. Goss describes the incident thusly. Our fighters had gotten separated in trying to make contact with the enemy and Goss was overtaking the formation from the rear as they started on their leaflet run over our airstrip.

"He was closing in, and actually had the bomber in his gunsight, when, before he had a chance to pull the trigger, the bomber exploded in the characteristically spectacular manner the Japanese aircraft had when six 50-caliber machine guns registered a direct hit. While the squadron commander was coming up for a shot from the rear, Hampshire approached the enemy fighters from directly ahead and picked their bomber right from the center of the protection of the Imperial Japanese Fighter Command. The 'world's finest fighter pilots' also lost some Zeroes that day and although we lost Lt. Berle Barnum, it was a good contest. I don't know whether the Japanese considered it a fair fight but they never tried another leaflet raid.

"Approximately three weeks after this incident I had an opportunity to spend a few days with the squadron. At this time I was the deputy group commander. Major Goss had received a special assignment from General Chennault and I had the good fortune of replacing him on a temporary basis which gave me an opportunity to spend a few days with the troops of the 75th. Flying and fighting with a group of men for almost a year develops a strong attachment. I looked forward to this visit with great anticipation.

"I had been with the squadron only a day or two when our telephone air raid warning net reported a group of 47 Zeroes approaching our airdrome. During the previous few days we had been sitting around telling each other how good we were, perhaps stretching the truth a little. I'm sure we weren't nearly so good as we thought we were but it is terribly important for the fighter pilot to feel that way about his business. Hampshire had a great sense of humor and was always kidding.

"The Japanese employed a peculiar squirrel cage kind of formation when they made a fighter attack on our airdromes and on this occasion Hampshire stated his intent to join the formation and not come out until he either broke it up or was shot down. He then invited me to join him and made me a wager that I would chicken out before he did. He was kidding me about this as we walked out to our airplanes and took off as the warning net reported the 47 airplanes coming down from the north.

"On this day the 75th squadron had 16 airplanes in commission manned by pilots seasoned with almost a year of combat. Sixteen P-40's with expert pilots against only 47 Zeroes appeared to us to be kind of unfair because in the earliest days of the war we had been outnumbered sometimes as high as ten to one. On this day we were all in good spirits and anticipated giving the Japs a resounding beating.

"I positioned the 16 airplanes above and to one side of our airdrome at 18,000 feet. I don't know what happened to the Japanese formation but the 47 aircraft stopped some distance away and 10 or 15 came forward on a reconnaissance. They crossed our airdrome at about 5,000 feet below us and I thought this must be a trap. I waited for a few minutes until reports from the warning net indicated that the rest of the formation was not going to commit itself and then we attacked. Either my aim was poor or the Japanese pilot I engaged was skillful, because I failed to score after expending considerable ammunition. Everyone became scattered in the melee and then five of the pilots assembled on my wing and I started north to engage the main body of the formation which, according to reports, was retreating back to Hankow. In-flight reports told of about 5 or 6 Zeroes claimed in the action. Hampshire came up on my wing and reported one kill and stated that I could find the wreckage one mile north off the north end of our runway—and there it was when we went out to investigate. This was Hampshire's fifth air-to-air fight and this airplane was his 13th victory. Although his life was ended a few short minutes later, I was able to confirm his 14th victory in his fifth air-to-air engagement before a lucky or a skillful shot ended his life.

"As I led my small formation north there was lots of excitement and chatter on the radio. Hampshire, kidding as always, was wagering I would never overtake the Japanese. About 100 miles north of our airfield I encountered a huge thunderstorm and I let down to about 500 feet to pass underneath it. As I let down, I saw three Zeroes hugging the ether ahead and making for home. I said a few words of constraint to the five pilots with me, hoping they would stay back and let me get a shot. As we bored in, Hampshire went underneath and pulled up in front of me while I was firing and we both missed the leader of the enemy formation; however, his two wing men who were tucked in tight both hit the ground simultaneously.

"It was a spectacular start and I was so intent on the three sitting ducks that I failed to see a larger formation of Japanese above us. They attacked: there was adequate confusion and lots of screams and laughter on the radio. It was over in a few short minutes and we re-formed to return to our base. When we counted noses Hampshire was missing.

"We were fighting over the edge of a broad river which emptied into a lake near the city of Changsha. One of our pilots had seen an aircraft dive vertically into the lake: another one contradicted this and stated that the airplane had landed in the water near the river bank and that the aircraft looked as though it were a P-40. There was some confusion, as the pilot who saw the aircraft go vertically into the water was sure it was a Zero while the pilot who saw the aircraft land in the water felt that it was a P-40.

"The confusion was cleared up shortly after we landed at our own base. I received a wire from the Chinese command post in the Changsha area. It was brief and shocking. Overcoming the difficulties in a manner of expression, the wire said simply: 'American pilot landed in river. Hit in stomach, guts running out. Send doctor quick.'

"I don't have the talent or the understanding to explain the emotion that went through the hearts of John Hampshire's friends. One of his most devoted friends was our flight surgeon, Ray Spritzler, who announced that he was going to John's assistance. The matter of transporting him was solved when someone suggested that we stuff him in the baggage compartment of one of our fighters and have him jump out in the vicinity of where John went down. At this time and under the stress and emotion I did not realize how hazardous and how foolish such a venture might be. I consented and we made the doctor as comfortable as possible in the uncomfortable and cramped quarters of a fighter baggage compartment which was not designed to accommodate a human being. The door was removed and a signal arranged between the pilot, Lt. Joe Griffins, and Ray which would tell the doctor when he was over the proper area. A signal such as wobbling the wings or shaking the aircraft had to be used for there was no way for the pilot and doctor to communicate.

"We saw them off and it was not until they departed into the northern sky where storms had begun to gather that I think I realized this might not be a good idea. I grew truly fearful when, a few minutes after their departure, we received a second wire from the Chinese stating that Hampshire had died. We tried to reach Griffins on the radio but electrical disturbances caused by thunder squalls to the north made this impossible.

"I spent an anxious hour or so waiting for them to return and finally just at dark we got a report from our warning net that a lone airplane was approaching the vicinity of our airport. At this time we did not know it, but Griffins had run into severe weather and had been unable to reach Changsha and the doctor was still stuffed in the baggage compartment of the fighter.

"Our warning net, although it gave us excellent intelligence, was often not exact and after dark landmarks on the Chinese countryside were not distinguishable. In this part of China there were no electrical systems or electric lights. Our runway was outlined with a thin row of smudge pots fueled by tung oil. Their feeble light would give a pilot the outline of the runway for landing but they could not be seen much more than a mile from the airport.

"We heard Griffins' airplane droning through the dark and although we tried to reach him on the radio and give him directions, the intensity of the static made this impossible. Hours passed and there were no reports. I computed the time when they would run out of fuel and after this my heart really sank. I composed a wire to Chennault stating that I had lost Hampshire, but I didn't have the courage to tell him that I had lost another airplane and possibly another good pilot and my doctor because of my own poor judgment. I decided to wait out the night as I was in hopes that before morning we would have a report as to where the airplane had crashed and I was hoping for some miracle to insure the safety of two good friends who were risking their lives for another good friend whom they couldn't save. I prayed for forgiveness for my stupidity and I prayed for a little help.

"Morning came and still no word and several hours after we had manned our aircraft down on the flight line I decided that I had no alternative to letting General Chennault know how stupid I had been. I was composing my wire when someone shouted "Here they come" and a fighter airplane touched down on the airfield and taxied up to the line. When it swung around everybody could see the doctor's face sticking out of the baggage compartment, grinning from ear to ear.

"What had happened was almost incredible. The night before they had been completely lost and Griffins, the pilot, almost out of gas, had made the decision to abandon the airplane. Before he gave the signal to jump he happened to spy a cluster of small lights on the ground. Because there was no electricity, any group of small lights probably meant a village. Joe reasoned that there might be a telephone in the village and that if he circled it, this would be reported to the Chinese warning net and at least we at the base would have a fix on where he and the doctor had abandoned their aircraft.

"As he circled the group of lights he noticed to his amazement a long stream of fire flare up nearby. He went over to investigate and it was apparent from the pattern of the flames that the Chinese below had set fire to a field, expecting him to land. He quickly lowered his landing gear because there was precious little fuel remaining, lined up with the flames and put his airplane down not knowing whether there were holes or rough spots or barriers artificial or otherwise. To his amazement he hit in a smooth area and the airplane rolled to a stop without incident.

"When he dismounted from the cockpit he found himself in the hands of friendly Chinese who were overjoyed to see him. This particular village had an old abandoned emergency airstrip of which we had absolutely no knowledge. The Chinese are a smart people and when they heard the aircraft circling overhead knew the pilot was in trouble. Quickwittedly, they opened a drum of aviation gasoline and rolled it down the center of the airstrip and then set fire to the spilled gasoline forming a more than adequate night lighting system for Griffins' approach. Ray Spritzler and Joe Griffins spent a thankful night with the Chinese and the next morning, after refueling from an emergency cache of gasoline, they set out for home. The reason we didn't hear from them was because this village was completely out of communication with the outside world.

"Looking back, I can distinguish between the foolish and the brave. It is of no use to dwell on how you would behave if you had to do it over because the chance will never come. I remember John Hampshire for the brave and wonderful man that he was. I remember the doctor who was perhaps even braver in a different way, and how Joe Griffins and the doctor made futile plans to help a good friend who was beyond help. I have great pride in these men and their memories and in spite of our mistakes I don't think even if we had the chance to do it over again we'd do it any differently."

Chapter 18

By the end of the summer of 1942, the lack of supplies had begun to have a telling effect. All of the P-40 Allison engines were long overdue on major overhaul. But they were running on engine oil that had been filtered and used over and over again. Only four-ply tires were available and the rocky China air strips cut them to ribbons. Many pilots made combat flights with tail wheel casings stuffed with rags. Many of the plane engines had run for 300 hours without proper repair. Carburetors were so worn that the automatic fuel mixture controls would not work.

These obviously were very serious matters for the men to contend with, for they not alone faced death from the enemy, but death from their own worn-out equipment. In early September a pilot received severe shocks when an electrical system on a P-40 short-circuited. Another pilot had a Japanese plane in his gun sight when the electrical system failed and the gun did not fire. Another pilot made a crash landing in the midst of a fight because his engine quit in mid-air. All of these failures were due to wear and tear without replacement of worn parts.

By late September the CATF was down to thirty-eight pilots for thirty-four flyable P-40's, with only two days' gas left. As General Chennault wrote, "The China Air Task Force, unbroken in combat, was facing death from acute starvation."

During the fall, things improved. Bombing planes, worn P-40K fighters and twenty splendid fighter pilots seasoned by a year of flying P-40's in Panama arrived. Of this group Chennault said, "This group of Panama post-graduates produced some of the finest pilots ever to fight in China. Their names— Hampshire, Pryor, Wilcon, Richardson, Brookfield, Blackstone, Little, Tempest, Gordon, Grosvenor and Stewart—studded the combat reports."

Before the dismal weather of December, combined with the lack of supplies, kept the CATF grounded and made Chennault sick with acute bronchitis and influenza, the CATF gave a good account of itself during the good fall weather. There were many signs during October that the Japanese were preparing heavy blows against the supply line over the Himalayas. Reconnaissance over French Indo-China in September showed an increase in enemy fighter strength around Hanoi.

There were also many signs of renewed ground activity on the Salween front. This, of course, indicated that the Japanese might attempt to follow the aerial blows they obviously were staging with a crossing of the Salween in sufficient force to drive successfully toward Kunming. The CATF, however, was able to keep the enemy supply system sufficiently off balance to make it impossible to accumulate enough material in strategic positions to launch a major offensive. Never were the Japanese able to support more than a few small patrols on the East bank of the Salween River, and their long-planned major offensive never materialized despite the weakness of the Chinese defending forces.

The CATF fighters specialized in short bombing and strafing runs, which enabled it to keep fighting even on the fast dwindling supplies available at the Yunnan fields. The air as far south as Lashio was ruled by the CATF.

General Chennault gave great attention to possible ways of luring the new, fast Japanese fighters into the limited destructive range of the P-40's. All of the Jap planes—the Oscars, twin-engined Nicks, and the new clipped-wing Zero known as the Hamp—all had enormous altitude advantage over the P-40, combined with a superior rate of climb. The P-40 operated at its maximum efficiency between 15,000 and 18,-000 feet. At any altitude above 20,000 feet it rapidly lost efficiency. General Chennault's plan was to use his 11th Squadron bombers as bait, sending them in on a bomb run at 15,000 feet with P-40's stacked above to 18,000 feet. Thus, in order to close on the bombers, the Japanese fighters would have to lose their altitude advantage and come within range of the P-40's at the American planes' best fighting altitude.

It was obvious that to lure the Japanese into such a trap, the CATF would need to strike toward a target so important that the Japanese could not afford to leave it undefended. The target finally selected was Hong Kong. Caleb Haynes, of whom my husband said, "He often reminded me of a gorilla, but he flew like an angel," was particularly keen to bomb Hong

Kong. The Japanese radio had been repeating a scornful message that its listeners had little to fear from American bombers because they were led by "an old broken-down transport pilot named Haynes." Caleb Haynes smarted under these thrusts and at his own expense had large quantities of leaflets printed in English and Japanese to the effect that "These bombs come with the compliments of the old broken down transport pilot Haynes."

On October 24, the CATF attack force left Kweilin. It consisted of twelve B-25's and ten P-40's and the next morning this force dropped the first Allied bombs on Hong Kong. Fighter cover was led by "Tex" Hill and Caleb Haynes led the bombers. Colonel Merian Cooper was in the nose of Haynes' B-25, peering over the shoulder of Harold "Butch" Morgan.

The attack was a complete surprise and a complete success. The bombs and Haynes' leaflets came fluttering down before the enemy fighters could rise to attack. Twenty-six Japanese fighters rose and were about to dive on the homeward-bound American bombers when the P-40's pounced on them out of the sun like screaming, plummeting eagles. In a running fight, the CATF lost one bomber and both Chinese intelligence and the Japanese radio carried the Japanese casualty list at twenty downed Jap planes between Canton and Hong Kong.

It was General Chennault's plan to continue to smash at the ships and docks around Hong Kong until gas and bombs were exhausted. This was not to be. At 1 A.M. a message reached Chennault from Bissell in Delhi. "Bomb Lashio and Myitkyina airdromes until further notice beginning at dawn."

Chennault was despondent. Lashio and Myitkyina were 800 miles away. Half of his bombers were in the air, the other half gassed and ready to smash at the tempting and overripe targets in Hong Kong. Chennault guessed what had happened. Despite the early warning messages of the enemy buildup in Burma, which Chennault had sent to Bissell, he had been caught with his planes down. Only two of the twenty P-40's on the field were able to get into the air. Twelve P-40's and ten DC-3's, over half the entire Hum air transport force, were destroyed on the ground.

Knowing that to bomb the obviously empty Japanese fields at Lashio and Myitkyina was futile, Chennault obeyed orders. He radioed the lone B-25 at Kunming to bomb Lashio at dawn. The remainder of the Mitchells joined in this futile effort. Nevertheless, Chennault did bomb Hong Kong. He loaded every available P-40 with a 500-pound bomb, and against heavy flack and determined Jap fighter attacks, the P-40's dive-bombed shipping in Victoria Harbor. They managed to sink a tanker and several freighters.

In December the CATF was grounded because of weather and lack of supplies. Chennault himself was grounded continually from acute bronchitis and influenza. Only the able and constant attention of his personal physician, Colonel Tom Gentry, kept him, most of the time, on his feet. But often, eyes bright and legs weak from fever and his chest wracked by coughing, Chennault continued to direct the operations of his forces and, sick or not, he travelled from airfield to airfield in the rickety old Beechcraft.

During the winter, Chennault and Bissell exchanged bitter, angry "eyes alone" messages over the lack of the common necessities of any group of Americans in a theater of war—what the British called the "amenities."

Bissell, without good reason, failed the CATF on such essentials as mail, warm clothing, soap, razorblades, cigarettes, promotions, and decorations for valor in combat. For two to three months at a time post-exchange supplies were undelivered, leaving the CATF without a whole bar of soap, razor blades, or cigarettes. Nevertheless, the precious DC-3 transports were regularly sent to theater headquarters in Chungking with the monthly five-ton load of canned food, beer, cigarettes, and auto gas.

During one stretch of bad weather when morale sagged low because of the lack of mail for three weeks, Chennault sent a DC-3 over the Hump with orders to bring back the mail sacks. When it returned loaded with tennis shoes for the Chinese army Chennault considered the profanity heard around the alert shacks justified.

In the absence of woolen clothes requisitioned

from India, the men bought horsehide jackets and fur hats in Kunming markets. Patched pants became the true insignia of the CATF—yet Bissell continued to complain about the non-regulation attire of Chennault's men.

Bissell steadfastly turned down Chennault's recommendations for medals for CATF personnel for gallantry in action, on the ground that the incidents cited were in the line of duty. He capped this by rejecting a posthumous Silver Star, a high combat decoration, for Captain P. B. O'Connell who dive-bombed and sank a tanker in Hong Kong Harbor in the face of enemy fighter attacks which cost his life. Bissell informed Chennault that he, sitting in Delhi, was a better judge of a fighter pilot's condition than Chennault and forced Ed Rector and "Tex" Hill to stay in China an extra month despite the fact that both were ill with malaria and dysentery and had flown in continuous combat for one year. With remarkable restraint and understatement, my husband recorded in his diary:

As a result of all this. Bissell was not the most popular man in China. CATF fighter pilots sitting on clay revetments beside an alert shack whiled away long hours between flights dreaming up elaborate insults to 10th Air Force staff officers living on "Per Diem" Hill in Delhi. Their choice barbs were naturally reserved for Bissell. At Kunming they taught Chinese coolies to carry cargo and passenger baggage from transports to greet new arrivals with what can be politely translated as 'Nuts to Bissell.' This, the fighter boys assured the coolies, was a standard American greeting. The coolies, pleased with their knowledge, religiously greeted each transport with a resounding chorus of 'Nuts to Bissell.' This was great sport for the browned-off fighter boys until one day when General Bissell stepped off the transport in Kunming and was greeted by the grinning coolies shouting 'Nuts to Bissell!' He was not amused.

The most serious problem faced by the CATF was the failure of Stilwell and Bissell to meet supply quotas for the CATF. They had agreed to provide the CATF with a monthly tonnage of 1,986 tons by air over the Hump. But by January 1943 the CATF was getting only 300 tons a month; in February, 400 tons; and in March, out of an allocation of 1,000 tons, only 615 tons arrived.

General Chennault could understand Stilwell's ignorance of the airlift potential but he could never understand why Bissell, an airman, considered the Hump operation impractical. Nevertheless, Bissell maintained that to deliver 5,000 tons a month to Kunming from India would require a fleet of 300 transports and twenty-five airfields. But less than a year after this estimate, the Air Transport Command was delivering 10,000 tons a month to Kunming, using only 150 transport planes.

But the CATF kept fighting, making the most of

what it had to work with and fight with. But the end due to lack of supplies was rapidly approaching.

On Christmas Day, 1942, the Japanese attacked Yunnanyi. They tried again the next day but were intercepted by four P-40's over the Mekong River and lost five bombers and three fighters. This fight left Yunnanyi completely devoid of gasoline and for the rest of the winter the CATF was hard pressed to obtain enough gasoline to keep the radio station generator in operation. At Kunming, gas supplies were so low that General Chennault barred all buzzing and victory rolls after combat missions. A few strafing missions were launched over Burma in January, but after that for thirty-three maddening, frustrating days the CATF planes were grounded because of the lack of gasoline.

Chapter 19

During the dark winter of 1942-1943, while Chinese resistance to overpowering Japanese military strength slowly crumbled, Chennault wrote two documents which are remarkable for their forthrightness and importance in the history of World War II.

In the first of these documents, a memorandum to Stilwell, dated August 13, 1942, General Chennault informed the CBI theater commander that American military inactivity, combined with the failure to provide air support to the Chinese armies constituted the "gravest danger" to the war effort in China. He urgently recommended that he be given a "small, effective air force" consisting of five hundred bombers and fighter planes, one hundred transport planes to fly supplies over the Himalayas, and "complete authority over all air operations in China." If these requests were granted, Chennault promised to relieve pressure on General MacArthur in the South Pacific, neutralize Japan's air efforts over Burma, Indo-China and India, and mount a successful air offensive against the Japanese in Asia.

Chennault informed Stilwell that immediate action was imperative and urged the theater commander to forward the text of his message to the Pentagon in Washington. But if either General George Marshall or "Hap" Arnold ever received copies of this message, Chennault never knew of it.

The second important document did reach Washington. It was drafted while Chennault directed the efforts of his China Air Task Force over East China. And the effects of his message, although a little slow in coming, eventually surprised and elated the Flying Tiger. In this paper, Chennault gave his honest, courageous and brutally frank evaluation of, firstly, the earthbound campaign-planning of the foremost American military leaders, which he branded "unrealistic." On the other hand, Chennault, without false modesty, but speaking from the courage of his proven convictions and his record of unbroken air successes in China, guaranteed victory over Japan— provided he were given supreme military command in China. He pointed out that his particular brand of war was air warfare but to wage it successfully he must have unhampered command of all offensive operations, including ground operations, in China. It is worthy of note, incidentally, that in this document Chennault once and for all underlined his concepts of successful air-ground warfare. Nowhere in it did he promise victory from air power alone, although his enemies in Washington later spread the canard that he had promised this. On the contrary, he knew very well that the positions gained and the successes won by air power would have to be consolidated, and held, by adequate ground forces. The ground forces, in turn, had to be protected by air power.

The letter was one that Chennault had thought of writing but had not written until asked to do so by

Wendell Willkie, President Roosevelt's personal
envoy who suggested such a letter, following a confidential talk with the Commander of the China Air
Task Force early in October 1942.

Willkie, possibly prompted by Roosevelt, sent
Chennault a message asking to talk to him. Chennault
replied that he could not see an official visitor without the approval of General Stilwell. The next day
Stilwell and Willkie motored to Peishiyi Airfield in
Stilwell's staff car. In the presence of Willkie, the
President's personal emissary, Stilwell had little
choice but to tell Chennault that he was free to talk
to the visitor about anything he wished. Then, with
Stilwell, the commanding officer of the CBI, waiting alone in an outer office of Chennault's headquarters, his subordinate and Wendell Willkie talked
for two hours.

Willkie was stunned at what he learned. Chennault
informed him that the Task Force was defending
China with fewer than fifty flyable fighter airplanes
and fewer than a dozen bombing planes. Willkie
learned, to his amazement, that the well-publicized,
large-scale assaults by big fleets of U.S. airplanes in
China were distorted Stateside interpretations. Instead, Chennault informed Willkie, such "large-scale
raids" were actually tiny, savage, hit-and-run forays
which usually were carried out with fewer than
twenty wornout, patched-up airplanes operating on
minuscule gasoline rations. Censorship, Chennault
pointed out, was the device employed to hide the

incredible poverty of air warfare resources in China. At Willkie's obvious question, "Why?" Chennault reluctantly admitted that this portion of his trouble was caused by Tenth Air Force and theater command neglect and indifference of Bissell's Tenth Air Force and China Theater Command, which he concluded were about to reduce the air warfare potential in China to the point of virtual ineffectiveness.

It was after hearing this, that Willkie, shocked, asked Chennault to state the entire situation in a frank, detailed letter addressed to the President of the United States as Commander-in-Chief. He told Chennault that he wanted to take the letter to the White House in person. In response to this request, Chennault prepared his letter of October 8, a paper which, coming from a subordinate military officer in a war theater, has probably never been excelled or equalled for sheer audacity or for the magnitude of its scope. And although Commander-in-Chief Roosevelt had asked for the letter, this is why after Roosevelt died, the bureaucracy removed Chennault from his command in China, in the same uncomprehending way that it court martialed another airman who was right, Billy Mitchell.

Chennault worked most of one night preparing the long, detailed letter which was dispatched to Chengtu by air courier in the morning to catch Willkie. This remarkable letter, which provides so keen an insight into the tremendous inner confidence of my husband and his complete and detailed grasp of the factual

Maj. Gen. Chennault and Brig. Gen. Edgar E. Glenn inspect engine repair on a Curtiss P-40 "Warhawk" at an airfield in Kunming, China, November 3rd, 1944.

How the 14th Air Force got gas.

ramifications of the war in China as he saw them, and about which history now shows him to have been right, is reproduced here, in full:

October 8, 1942

Mr. Wendell Willkie,
Special Representative of the President
In his capacity as Commander-in-Chief
of the Armed Forces.

You have stated to me that you are the direct representative in a military, as well as a political sense, of the Commander-in-Chief of the United States Army, the President of the United States. You have ordered me to make a report directly to you on military operations in China against Japan. I herewith comply.

1. Japan can be defeated in China.

2. It can be defeated by an Air Force so small that in other theaters it would be called ridiculous.

3. I am confident that, given real authority in command of such an Air Force, I can cause the collapse of Japan. I believe I can do it in such a manner that the lives of hundreds of thousands of American soldiers and sailors will be saved, and that the cost to our country will be relatively small.

4. I speak with confidence, but, I believe, not with egotism. The reason for my confidence is based on the fact that since 1923 I have believed firmly in the possibility of Japan making war on the United States; I have devoted the best years of my military life to the study of this subject; I have for five years been unofficial adviser to the Chinese Air Force; in this capacity, I made war against Japan for over five years; for the last year I have commanded first the

A. V. G., then the China Air Task Force; at no time in China have I had as many as fifty fighting planes in operation to meet the full fighting air force of Japan; as Commander of the A. V. G. and the China Air Task Force, I have never lost an air battle against the Japanese .This tiny fighter force under my Command has destroyed over three hundred Japanese aircraft confirmed and about three hundred more probably destroyed—I believe the total to be about six hundred—with the loss of twelve A. V. G. pilots and Four China Air Task Force pilots from enemy action. The bomber force of the China Air Task Force has consisted at maximum of eight medium bombers. With these I have made twenty-five raids against Japanese installations, troops, and shipping, without the loss of either a man or plane through enemy action.

5. When I came to China the Chinese Air Force was under Italian advisers. Before America entered the war I had succeeded (because I believed we would fight the Axis powers and Japan), in having the Italians sent out of China. I believe I have the full confidence of the Generalissimo and all high Chinese leaders. If I have their confidence it is because (a) I have been a winning general, (b) I have never lied to the Chinese, and I have never promised to perform more than I believed capable of performance.

6. I am now confident that given full authority as the American military commander in China that I can not only bring about the downfall of Japan but that I can make the Chinese lasting friends with the United States. I am confident that I can create such good will that China will be a great and friendly trade market for generations.

7. The military task is a simple one. It has been complicated by unwieldy, illogical military organization and by men who do not understand aerial warfare in China.

8. To accomplish the downfall of Japan, I need only this very small American Air Force—105 fighter aircraft of modern design, 30 medium bombers, and in the last phase, some months from now, 12 heavy bombers. The force must be constantly maintained at all times. We will have losses. These losses must be replaced. I consider 30 per cent replacements in fighters and 20 per cent in bombers sufficient.

9. My reason for stating that I can accomplish the overthrow of Japan is that I am confident this force can destroy the effectiveness of the Japanese Air Force, probably within six months, within one year at the outside. I am a professional fighter and his is my professional opinion. The facts on which this opinion is based are simple. Japan has only a limited production of aircraft. I can force that Japanese Air Force by aerial military maneuver to fight me in a position of my own selection. Having once fixed it in this position I can destroy its effectiveness. With its basic effective Air Force destroyed, our Navy can operate with freedom, and General MacArthur can push his offensive in the South West Pacific at will. Meanwhile, from the Eastern Chinese Air Bases, I will guarantee to destroy the principal industrial centers of Japan. No country is so peculiarly vulnerable to air attack. The cutting of the Japanese sea route to her newly conquered empire is a simple matter. Once the above two objectives are accomplished the complete military subjection of Japan is certain and easy.

10. To effectively maintain the small air force

mentioned above, an aerial supply line must be built up between India and China. It is a simple statement of fact to say this aerial supply line will also be minute compared to the objectives to be accomplished. The full establishment and maintenance of this aerial ferry route is child's play in comparison with the difficulties overcome in establishing the Pan American-South American air line or its Atlantic and Pacific air lines. It only needs good command— good management. The amount of freight to be carried over this air line in order to maintain an air force is very small—the accompanying study will state the basic simplicity.

11. The present plan for the defense of this ferry line is that of the standard orthodox, rigid military mind. It has no real military value. It shows complete lack of conception of the true use of air power or even of basic military strategy. I would defend this air line in the same way that Scipio Africanus defended Rome, when Hannibal was at its very gates. Scipio struck at Carthage, and the Carthaginians, by necessity, had to call Hannibal and his Army back to Africa to defend Carthage. In like manner, I would defend the ferry route by striking at the Japanese supply lines to the Southwest Pacific, and then hit Tokyo itself. The Japanese Air Force by necessity would then be forced to fight in Eastern China and over Tokyo. The Japanese have not the air power to fight both over the ferry route in India, Burma and Yunnan, and over Tokyo at the same time. No capable commander in history has ever adopted the stolid plan of the present method of defending the ferry route. Grant ordered Sherman to march through the heart of the South and destroy Lee's supplies and cut Lee's lines of communications while,

he, Grant, fixed Lee's Army in northern Virginia. Once Lee's supplies and lines of communications were cut, Lee was defeated and the Confederacy was ruined. I plan to do the same thing in China against Japan with air power. Japan must hold Hong Kong, Shanghai, and the Yangtze Valley. These are essential to hold Japan itself. I can force the Japanese Air Force to fight in the defense of these objectives behind the best air warning net of its kind in the world. With the use of these tactics, I am confident that I can destroy Japanese aircraft at the rate of between ten and twenty to one. When the Japanese Air force refuses to come within my warning net and fight, I will strike out with my medium bombers against their sea supply line to the Southwest Pacific. In a few months the enemy will lose so many aircraft that the aerial defense of Japan will be negligible. I can then strike at Japan from Chuchow (Chuhsien) and Lishui with heavy bombers. My air force can burn up Japan's two main industrial areas —Tokyo and the Kobe, Osaka, Nagoya triangle— and Japan will be unable to supply her armies in her newly conquered empire in China, Malaya, the Dutch East Indies, etc. with munitions of war. The road is then open for the Chinese Army in China, for the American Navy in the Pacific and for MacArthur to advance from his Australian stronghold—all with comparatively slight cost.

12. While engaged in these operations, I will maintain full ground installations for the eastern terminus of the ferry route in Yunnan, at Kunming, Chanyi, Yunnanyi, etc. If a really major swift aerial movement is made by the Japanese across their staging route into Burma, to attack the India-China air supply lines, then, acting on interior lines of air

communications, I can move back and again be within the warning net which I have established in Yunnan, and meet the Japanese over their Burma airfields and then and there destroy whatever force they have sent against us.

My entire above plan is simple. It has been long thought out. I have spent five years developing an air warning net and radio command service to fight this way. I have no doubt of my success.

13. However, in order to accomplish this aim, it is essential that I be given complete freedom of fighting action, that I also be able to deal directly with the Generalissimo and the Chinese forces. This latter I know the Generalissimo desires. I would not make the above statements so confidently if I had not, in my operations with the A. V. G., never retreated one foot until the ground forces had fled behind me, leaving my air bases exposed to ground attack. Only then did I retreat to again destroy twenty Japanese planes for each one of the A. V. G. lost. Even then I would not have been forced to retreat if I had had the necessary bombers and reconnaissance planes.

Given authority to report only to the Generalissimo, I intend to carry out in China this combined ground and air action.

14. This plan I again repeat will enable the Chinese ground forces to operate successfully, and most assuredly will permit MacArthur to successfully advance and will decisively aid the Navy's operations in the Pacific. Moreover, it will make China our lasting friend for years after the war.

C. L. Chennault
Brigadier General, A. U. S.
Commanding.

Chennault's letter went from the White House to the Pentagon where it was immediately stamped "Top Secret" to keep its grave charges of myopic mismanagement from the public. It arrived in Washington at the time when T. V. Soong and Generalissimo Chiang Kai-shek in persistent cables to the President, were pounding away at the obvious necessity for a separate China Air Force and an adequate "Hump" supply line. The steady succession of Chinese complaints, combined with the shock effect of Chennault's letter, brought dramatic action within the space of a few months. On March 3, 1943, Claire Lee Chennault was promoted to Major General and on March 10 the China Air Task Force became the Fourteenth U. S. Air Force. Claire Chennault had finally broken free from the baleful influence of Clayton Bissell, commander of the Tenth Air Force, in India.

Despite its faltering beginning, and the starvation supply diet it had been fed, the CATF had chalked up an impressive combat record. During nine months of sporadic but inspired operations it had destroyed 149 enemy planes in the air and probably destroyed eighty-five additional, with a loss of sixteen P-40's. Only once had Japanese fighters been able to pierce the American fighter cover to shoot down a lone B-25 bomber. During the entire period the CATF was the only tangible evidence of the American force and American spirit to the millions of Chinese. Of the CATF, General Chennault has written: "The CATF was probably the smallest American Air Force ever to be dignified by the command of a general. It certainly was the raggedest. Its paper work was poor, and salutes were scarce, but when the signals were called for combat, it never missed a play."

Chapter 20

Following the creation of the Fourteenth Air Force, my husband was under no illusion that from now on his dealing with Lieutenant General Stilwell—still the boss of the China-Burma-India Theater—would be without discord. But at least he was now in command of his own air force and in a better position to fight back. A real advantage that immediately accrued was that Clayton Bissell could no longer direct combat operations. Although Bissell still controlled the vital Hump supply line, the military high command in the Pentagon could hardly dub its fighting arm in China an Air Force, yet refuse the commanding general a reasonably adequate staff and a reasonable number of airplanes.

All might not be well, but at least General Chennault's status had advanced and his effectiveness had improved, while his military stature had been elevated. It was no small satisfaction to Chennault that he who less than six years before had been invited to leave the Army wearing the slender bars of a captain now wore the two stars of a major general.

The one conceivable weakness Major General Chennault may have had as he stepped into command of a full-fledged air force, making him a mark for critics, was almost providentially solved for him, out of his eventful past.

Years before, when he had demonstrated the power of paratroops at Brooks Field, one junior officer had been impressed when his superiors were not: Lieutenant Colonel Fred C. Milner. Years later, when Chennault, in Washington to establish the AVG, called on General Hap Arnold, commanding the Army Air Corps, Arnold's Adjutant was Colonel Fred Milner.

General Arnold was not sympathetic with Chennault's "unorthodox" plans but Milner, remembering the paratrooper demonstration, was impressed with Chennault's personality and imagination. The success of the AVG had confirmed Colonel Milner's instinctive initial judgment of Chennault, and when the Fourteenth Air Force was finally formed, with Chennault commanding, Milner, wanting to get from behind a desk and into a combat theater, had only one choice—to join Chennault and the Fourteenth Air Force in China.

To get there, he spurned Arnold's offer of a general's star and another desk job—but he went. In China he masterfully obliterated General Chennault's only "weakness" as commander of a large military organization, his impatience with the formalities, records and paper work he knew were necessary. The entire organizational apparatus of the AVG, for instance, had consisted of three old filing cases converted from ammunition boxes, and a metal box for the paymaster. Even Clayton Bissell couldn't complain about **Colonel Milner!**

Now Chennault could hope, perhaps optimistically, that creation of the Fourteenth Air Force would at last give him the freedom, the authority and the necessary supplies with which he could conduct the type of air war which he knew could quickly drive the Japanese Air Force out of the skies over China.

The fates had indeed decreed that Chennault would drive the Japanese Air Force out of China's skies; he would do it with incredible speed—six brief months—but he was not going to be able to start those six months of success until many weary earlier months had passed and until Lieutenant General "Vinegar Joe" Stilwell, the CBI theater commander, had finally been sent home in October, 1944. Until Stilwell's ouster, the new Fourteenth Air Force would indeed chalk up an incredibly valorous fighting record with woefully inadequate supplies. It would never, however, reach peak combat effectiveness simply because planes must have gasoline to fly. General Stilwell, ably abetted by General Bissell, still sitting astride the supply line at the Indian terminus, in the course of the bitterest personal feud of World War II between high ranking military men, saw to it that Chennault never received anything approaching the level of what he needed to make his plans come true.

Stilwell, indeed, was in a "bind." It seems probable that he realized that if he were to give his subordinate, Chennault, all the supplies that the commander of the Fourteenth requested, two things might happen: first, the Fourteenth Air Force might so successfully harass the Japanese and block their advances, backed by adequate Chinese ground troops to consolidate and hold the territory won by the air force, that Stilwell would never receive supreme command of the ground forces of China which, if things went badly, he might demand; second, he would have been proved wrong in his low estimate of the potential of air power by his irritating, rebellious subordinate.

I want again to reiterate that I am not a military strategist, or indeed a military expert. I must, however, record that it was my husband's firm opinion that the deliberate orders of General Stilwell curtailing Fourteenth Air Force combat operations, combined with further orders withholding ammunition and supplies which the very able Chinese General Hsueh Yo sorely needed, contributed significantly to the 1944 defeat of the East China Armies by the Japanese. It is a further fact, my husband always maintained, that the terrible East China defeats came close to eliminating China once and for all as an effective World War II Allied combatant.

It is, furthermore, a matter of military fact that General Stilwell either deliberately disobeyed, or forgot, orders from the Pentagon, stemming from the White House, which gave General Chennault command over the Hump air supply line into China. In similar fashion, General Stilwell—or it may conceivably have been General Bissell, acting on his own initiative—ignored the clear and specific Hump tonnage priorities of the Fourteenth Air Force.

A further inglorious but incontrovertible military fact is that Stilwell's CBI heaquarters for unknown reasons saw fit to turn down all of Chennault's requests for rest facilities for his battle-fatigued combat men, although such rest-leaves were liberally authorized in the Vale of Cashmere and other restful spots, not only for fighting men in the Tenth Air Force but for non-combat personnel in that command and in the Air Transport Command. In addition, CBI headquarters refused to authorize a building addition as Chennault's staff outgrew its old AVG Kunming headquarters.

In both cases, Chennault was able to cope with the situation because of the cooperation of Chinese authorities. When his own American headquarters refused the necessary facilities, China provided them as a gift to the Fourteenth Air Force.

With the birth of his air force, Chennault settled down to an orderly working and living schedule for the first time in five years. His daily routine became somewhat more free from the melee of critical emergencies, each requiring his personal attention. No longer was he personally forced to stand alert seven days a week at dawn and dusk scanning the horizons with binoculars at the edge of an improvised air strip. For the first time in his China career, General Chennault had an organization and a staff. Heading his staff was Brigadier General Edgar E. ("Buzz") Glenn, a West Point graduate, who had been sent in to furnish the type of spit and polish which the high brass

thought was necessary even in the hit-and-run guerrilla type operations which Chennault had been con-
ducting in China.

Actually, Buzz quickly abandoned the surface trap-
pings of his West Point training, and was soon a
faithful member of the Chennault group which placed
a far higher premium upon combat results and off-
duty relaxation. It was the same formula for success
in this informal guerrilla-type chess board operation
that had paid great dividends for years in China.

In mid-March, 1943, a four-engine Liberator B-24
Group was assigned to the Fourteenth Air Force, thus
satisfying a long-held dream of Chennault's—his own
bomber air force.

Another gift from the Chinese helped to make
Chennault's life more pleasant now that he was commanding an air force. This was a comfortable tile-
roofed adobe cottage which overlooked the Kunming
airfield and headquarters. In the cottage with General
Chennault lived General Buzz Glenn, Colonel Tom
Gentry, who was now Chief Surgeon and Chennault's
personal physician, and Captain Joseph Alsop, the
already well-known newspaper columnist. Now that
so many years have passed it can also be revealed that
while Joe Alsop's duties were ostensibly those of
press officer, he was also an intelligence officer.

Only a few realized how valuable an aide Joe was.
He was not only an able intelligence officer; he was
also infinitely resourceful in performing delicate outside missions, from the day he first obtained vital tire

replacements from the British for the AVG. Joe was not only Chennault's most effective communications line, but also his wisest advisor in the General's relations with Joe's cousin, the President in Washington. When the General left Kunming, Joe flew home with him.

Completing the General's household, were two Chinese houseboys, Riley and Gunboat; the cook; and chauffeur Wang, the General's driver since 1938. Last, but by no means least, was the General's dearly beloved dog, Joe the dachshund. A battered Buick sedan served as the General's staff car. His personal plane was a patched-up twin-engined Douglas C-47 constructed by Chennault's field mechanics largely of salvagable odds and ends of crashed Hump transports.

All his life an early riser, Chennault's day in his office began at seven a.m., handling urgent radio messages to and from his wing and unit commanders. Afterward he held a general staff meeting and a tactical planning session with unit commanders and staff officers. The rest of the morning was occupied with the normal Army-type load of heavy paper work, i.e., reports, correspondence, etc. This heavy load of bureaucratic paper work was to Chennault the most disagreeable part of his work as a commanding officer.

"I have often been intrigued by the idea of a war from which paper was barred by mutual agreement," he once said.

Almost every day Chennault took an hour's nap after lunch, a habit of many years standing and which he credited for his ability to carry on a virtual round-the-clock regimen for so many years. After the nap, he would work on until seven p.m.

Such a schedule could prove deadening and sedentary but Chennault did not permit this to happen. Always an avid physical culture buff, at Kunming he organized sports—baseball, volley ball, badminton, and ping-pong for the entire establishment. He himself participated, and also continued to indulge in two lifelong hobbies—hunting and fishing. He was as successful in the good dove and duck country around Kunming as he had been in the woods and swamps of Louisiana and his table was usually graced with ducks, doves, pheasants, Burma geese and sand hill cranes in season. In his hunting expeditions he was ably assisted by his dachshund, Joe.

The dachshund is normally a below-the-ground hunting dog, a good badger dog with powerful digging paws with which to flush the burrowing quarry. Chennault, evidently as successful in teaching canines as he was humans, taught Joe to be an excellent retriever. Joe would willingly swim out in the coldest marsh water and retrieve a duck without a bruise. Joe had won his place in Chennault's life and heart by sheer ability and personality. He had been a gift from Col. John Williams, arriving in task force headquarters over Chennault's objections. But the little dog took to him immediately and vice versa, and Joe was soon a veteran air traveller, over the years compiling more air miles to his credit than many a seasoned aviator. Joe had the best bombing-raid nerves in Kunming. He thought that near hits of Japanese bombs were blasts from hunting shotguns and after a bomb fell nearby he would bark joyously as he eagerly rushed through the brush looking for fallen game.

This period at Kunming as commander of the U.S. Fourteenth Air Force was a comfortable one for Claire Lee Chennault. The cuisine in the cottage was excellent. Combined with the fruits of Chennault's hunting expeditions was the genius of Jerry Huang, a Columbia University Ph. D. with a flair for catering which resulted in the finest table food that the wartime surrounding area of China could afford.

The erstwhile commander of the Flying Tigers Group occupied about as safe a position as could be found in China. Kunming was at the center of an air-fighting web operating from Burma east to Formosa and from the Yangtze River south to the Tropic of Cancer.

Commanding all Fourteenth Air Force operations to the east and south of Kunming as far as the Indo-China border, was Brigadier General Casey Vincent. The 69th Wing, supporting ground forces along the Salween River and covering territory extending from Indo-China through Siam and Burma was commanded by Brigadier Jack Kennedy; the B-29 bases and other units in Szechwan and Shenshi Provinces to the north by Brigadier Russell E. Randall. Covering the gap between Randall's force to the north and Casey Vincent's force to the east was the Chinese-American composite wing commanded first by Brigadier General "Winnie" Morris and later by Colonel A. Bennett.

The group and squadron leaders of the Fourteenth were still youthful in years but by now so experienced in the Chennault brand of air combat tactics that their units often operated as independent air task forces. These stalwarts of the Fourteenth Air Force included Colonels Bruce Holloway, Tex Hill, Eddie Rector, Charlie Older, Bill Reed, Ed McComas, Harry Pike, John (Pappy) Herbst, Johnny Alison, and Jack Chennault, the General's eldest son. Among the almost equally experienced pilots of the Fourteenth were Major George McMillan, Phil Loofburrow, Ajax Baumler, Arthur Cruikshank, Elmer Richardson, Jim Bledsoe, Ed Goss, and others. Two members of this group Chennault described as "natural killers in combat": Pappy Herbst and Ed McComas, who achieved the rating of leading aces of the Fourteenth during their China service.

Supply continued to be the greatest single problem of the Fourteenth in China. Conditions would have been bad enough, with the best sort of CBI theater and Tenth Air Force cooperation, but in the atmosphere which prevailed, supply was in effect like a strangling noose. More exactly, it was the lack of vital supplies which made Chennault's operations so terribly difficult.

To begin with, and aside from the politics which had so great an effect upon the situation, the final distribution points for supplies in China were at the end of some 15,000 miles of the most fantastic supply line in the world. On top of this, the cargo-battle impact ratio was terrific. No less than eighteen tons of supplies had to arrive in an Indian port in order to drop a ton of bombs on Shanghai. Six gallons of gasoline were required to fuel the planes delivering a single gallon of gasoline to an advanced Fourteenth Air Force base.

On top of the 12,000-mile ocean voyage from the United States to Karachi and Bombay, the only open Indian ports, came the 1,500-mile journey across northern India over alternate, narrow-gauge and standard-gauge railways into the Assam Valley. At this point the Air Transport Command picked the supplies up for the 500-mile over-the-Hump airlift across the mighty Himalayas to the cluster of railheads in Yunnan Province.

Once in Yunnan, the supply cargo under optimum conditions travelled for eight additional weeks through a complex of railroads, rivers, and a 500-mile-long road which wound through the Kweichow mountains into the eastern air bases of the Fourteenth Air Force. A stoppage anywhere along this tortuous supply line would be reflected in the interruption of combat operations. There were plenty of stoppages.

After the summer of 1943, the trouble over the Hump was man-made, by Stilwell and Bissell. Neither was ever convinced that the Hump airlift was practical, in spite of the excellent record of the China

National Air Transport. The ultimate potential of the lift, proved by commanders who followed Bissell to be 13,000 tons a month, was never developed under Bissell and Stilwell. When operated to full capacity, later, after Bissell, the Hump airlift mechanism was at all times able to transport greater tonnages than the Assam-Bengal railroad and the Brahmaputra River barge lines could deliver to the Assam airfields.

But despite the supply problem, not a new one to Chennault, the commanding general of the Fourteenth Air Force maintained his hopes for a fast successful strike at the enemy as he whipped the Fourteenth into fighting shape. The enemy could not catch his planes on the ground because his far-flung air raid warning net was functioning well. His intelligence forces, networked into every Japanese occupied area, were sending word by portable radio and every other means every time the Japs made a move or began to prepare for one.

New airfields were being built in hours by hundreds of thousands of coolies, toiling with ant-like patience and persistence. These fields were being built against the planned raids of the heavy B-24 bombers and for the tremendous B-29's which were scheduled to arrive soon. Five years of Chennault's operations had created a well of gratitude and good relations that assured rescue operations for downed American pilots. Chennault now was ready for the showdown he knew was coming. He would face it with a real air combat force.

Chapter 21

My husband often remarked how odd it was that on the one hand, the rapport he enjoyed with so many men whom he met during the course of his career, and their confidence in him, increased the better they knew him; but that, on the other hand, with others the closer the association grew, the more bitterly they resented him, and the more violently they opposed him. In the case of the latter group, it always seemed that the more correct he proved to be, the greater became the resentment of those who had always opposed him.

During the so-called Trident Meeting of the Allied Combined Chiefs-of-Staff in Washington, D. C., during April and May of 1943, the supreme commander of the China-Burma-India theater of World War II, Lieutenant General Joseph Warren Stilwell suffered one of the most humiliating defeats of his life.

During this conference, attended by President Roosevelt, Prime Minister Churchill, and other world leaders, General Stilwell's plan for the prosecution of the war in China was rejected. Accepted in face-to-face discussion was the plan of his rebellious subordinate, Major General Claire Lee Chennault, Commander of the U. S. Fourteenth Air Force.

The result of this was a deterioration of the already strained relationship between Stilwell and Chennault.

So infuriated was Stilwell that he never accepted his defeat, and, once back at his post, never carried out the directives of the Conference. The tragic outcome of the whole affair was a series of Chinese defeats which almost eliminated one of the original "Big Five," China, from World War II.

The British were amused, the top echelon Pentagon "brass" angry with embarrassment, over the obvious split in the American delegation. Chennault, despite his victory, was far from happy. He had spoken honestly, but was so junior at the meeting that he did not rate an aide, much less a staff. He did not, in fact, even possess a complete regulation uniform and his seat at the August conferences was far to the rear, behind the resplendently uniformed and decoration-heavy American and British first-echelon representatives. No one ever asked his opinion until that of Stilwell, theater commander, had been heard. Thus he became, steadfastly, the lone dissenter in an American group of officers accustomed by unvarying custom to presenting a united front.

In the middle of a Stilwell discourse on the inferior quality of the Chinese leadership and his constant reiteration of "the Chinese soldiers won't fight," the President of the United States interrupted Stilwell with a point-blank question:

"What do you think of the Generalissimo?"

"He's a vacillating, tricky, undependable, old scoundrel who never keeps his word . . ." Stilwell began. The President again interrupted:

"Chennault, what do you think?"

"Sir," declared the commanding officer of the Fourteenth Air Force, "I think the Generalissimo is one of the two or three greatest military and political leaders in the world today. He has never broken a commitment or a promise made to me."

Never again was my husband invited by the United States military leaders to attend international conferences. He was present at the Cairo Conference, but only in his capacity as Air Force Chief-of-Staff to Generalissimo Chiang Kai-shek. This was after the Generalissimo failed in all-out efforts to have Chennault invited as a U. S. General.

Chennault sensed that for having been honest and outspoken at the Trident Conference, as he had always been throughout his life, he was now back in the same, familiar military dog house he had inhabited in the 1930's. It was now obvious that the penalty for courageous honesty was, ultimately, military oblivion. However excellent his plans might be for the winning of the war in China, as the "High Brass" saw things, the maintenance of iron military discipline was of greater importance than the winning of a world war. Chennault had committed the unpardonable military crime—insubordination.

The war plans which Chennault proposed at Trident were diametrically opposed to Stilwell's opposite concept. Stilwell, a sincere and courageous, but dyed-in-the-wool, infantryman championed a ground war against the jungle-proficient, well-dug-in Japanese in

Burma. Stilwell's plan was a simple one—based on well-conditioned men with sharp bayonets, mules and trucks operating in nearly impassible terrain, against a powerful enemy, able to subsist on one-fourth the American-required rations, and anxious for precisely such a contest. Chennault's plan, on the other hand, was substantively the one he had submitted to President Roosevelt in the letter hand-carried to the White House by Wendell Willkie. Briefly, it embodied a large-scale air offensive mounted in China and hurled against the vulnerable flank of the Japanese war efforts in the Pacific.

Stilwell, conversely, wanted to train an enormous number of Chinese infantry divisions in India, equipped with American arms, and instructed to fight their way south through heavy Japanese air and ground forces in the Burma jungle. Backing up his efforts, Stilwell desired American-trained Chinese divisions to attack on the Salween front and drive toward the Burma front which would then be opened by the India-based legions. The plan called on the British for an all-out attack spearheaded by an amphibious attack on Rangoon. Assuming this complex of ground assaults would prove successful, "Vinegar Joe" Stilwell wanted to train more Chinese in China, equip them with American arms and turn them toward the east China coast in order to open a receiving port for the American Navy in the Pacific. Nowhere in Stilwell's written plan, or in his blueprints, or in the arguments he made at the Trident Conference, was the word "airplane."

As Chennault said, later, in his memoirs, there was nothing much wrong with "Vinegar Joe's" plan except that by any stretch of the imagination, an optimistic estimate of its earliest completion was ten years hence. On the other hand, Chennault's plan called for fast action which he was certain would be carried out at a fraction of the expenditure of manpower, money and supply costs envisioned by the Stilwell program. It involved an intensive two-month operation against Japanese airpower, starting in July, followed by a secondary and decisive phase starting in September. Chennault was confident that such a program would place fire-bomb raids over Japanese cities by the end of 1943.

Chennault thought he had good reason to believe, as he did, that American fighter planes would be able to clear the China skies of Japanese planes in very short order, using far fewer pilots and airplanes than the Japanese. Japan's supply lifeline in the South Pacific—extending through the Taiwan Straits and the South China Sea—was already within easy range of the Fourteenth Air Force's medium bombers. In Japan proper, the production sources—Tokyo, Nagasaki, Kobi, Osaka, and Yokahama—were already within range of the China-based B-24 bombers. Chennault looked forward to pounding the China coastal ports of Hainan Island and the Gulf of Tonkin during the early phases of his anticipated air war.

Chennault planned to use his B-25 medium bombers to blast the Formosan Straits and the South China Sea, while his 308th heavy bombardment group began to bomb Taiwan and the Shanghai and Nanking area. He firmly believed that by the end of 1943 he could begin to bomb Japanese shipping from the southern part of Korea to Cam Ranh Bay in Indo-China and to strike simultaneously at the Japanese industrial islands of Honshu and Kyushu.

It is interesting that the only air strength requirement in the Chennault war plan was a mere one-hundred-fifty fighter planes, seventy medium bombers, thirty-five heavy bombers, and sufficient reserves to sustain this strength, plus a steady supply delivery across the Hump. Initially he wanted 4,790 tons of supplies a month, to build up gradually to an average monthly tonnage of 7,000-odd tons.

It is obvious, in his presentation at Trident and as later stipulated by him in detailed, revised plans, that he expected Chinese armies defending eastern China would be strengthened with American lend-lease weapons and equipment in order to facilitate closely coordinated operations between these ground forces and the Fourteenth Air Force. He believed that lend-lease would supply the Chinese ground armies with the small arms ammunition, the light artillery, machine guns and mortars which they obviously needed to carry on the war on the ground. Chennault could not anticipate that Stilwell would later oppose shipment of any American supplies at all to any Chinese units not under Stilwell's direct command. These are important points to remember in discussing Stilwell's later allegation that Chennault had promised to hold east China with air power alone. Chennault flatly denied this and cited his own written war plans to prove his point.

Contrary to normal army procedure, adoption of Chennault's plan for the war in China left Stilwell, as theater commander, charged with execution of a campaign which he had violently opposed. It was Stilwell's stubborn opposition—not only to Chennault's ideas but to the directive which he had received—plus Chennault's three private talks with President Roosevelt and one with Prime Minister Churchill, that implanted in General George Marshall's mind the ill-founded but deep suspicion that Chennault had intrigued against Stilwell. Actually, the shoe was on the other foot. It appears, now, that despite the Allied will as represented by President Roosevelt and Prime Minister Churchill, and agreed to by the military high commands of both of these great allies, Stilwell nevertheless was able to thwart the Allied will and by venting his spleen on Chennault, very nearly brought about a terrible debacle in China.

Chennault had found President Roosevelt deeply shocked at the true size of the tiny air force operating in China before creation of the Fourteenth Air Force. He also found, significantly, that President Roosevelt had trouble getting true facts from his immediate subordinates. The President had always been a true friend of China, an admirer of Chiang Kai-shek and was determined to keep China in the war. The President, however, while clearly aware of the strategic impact which air strikes on Japanese shipping and the Formosa Straits and South China Sea would have on the Japanese war effort, was not aware of how nearly impossible it was for Chennault, the general in charge, to carry out operations which he clearly could have carried out, and well, had he not been deliberately starved of the necessary supplies.

It is an astonishing and, I think, tragic commentary that the President of the United States, in his wartime capacity of Commander-in-Chief of our armed forces, was thwarted in exercising what he rightly believed to be within his power: the bolstering of Chennault's striking power in China. The President, obviously, was prevented from helping Chennault because of the intervention of two powerful subordinates. The first, obviously, was "Vinegar Joe" Stilwell. Second was Stilwell's superior, General Marshall, who as an old friend of Joe Stilwell, saw fit to support him in direct opposition not only to the President of the United States but to the plain facts which were available and which had been graphically described and pinpointed by General Chennault. However, for whatever reason, General Marshall chose to regard Chennault's opinions which had been directed by the President, and by the President's emissary, Wendell Willkie, as constituting a deliberate undermining of a superior officer, Stilwell. It is to me a sad commentary that an unwritten law—a law that decrees that a subordinate must choke back his convictions and support his superiors—must be held inviolate. Because here was a case where a brilliant subordinate was later proved right by history, and a plodding superior officer was later proved terribly, tragically wrong by history. Faced with this dilemma, the superior officer of both men, General Marshall, chose inexplicably to support the higher ranking of the two, the theater commander, at the expense of a great wartime ally of the United States, and ultimately, at the expense of the entire war effort of the people of the United States.

I have always felt, privately, that General Bissell, who dogged my husband's footsteps for so many years, was influential in turning General Stilwell against my husband. And that, in turn, General Marshall was merely being a "good soldier" in upholding General Stilwell, the three-Star General, the CBI Theater Commander, against "insubordination" by my brilliant genius, Claire Chennault.

But these things have a way of shaking down as the years unfold. History, I am sure, will record the true story.

Chapter 22

For the Japanese high command in Tokyo, the Allied move to build up their air strength in China conveyed a clear and alarming implication. The Japanese had had trouble enough with the small-scale AVG and CATF. Now, they almost instantly swung into action to try to counter the air force buildup.

Japanese ground troops struck on the west bank of the Yangtze near Ichang at the same time that an assault was launched by the Burma-based Japanese Air Force upon all of the South China air-supply terminals. Both Japanese moves came before the return of Chennault from Washington.

Brigadier General Buzz Glenn, commanding in Chennault's absence, capably shuttled his fighters between the Yangtze fighting front in the north and the Hump bases in the south so rapidly that in the north the combined effect of Chinese ground forces and the strafing of the Fourteenth Fighters turned the Chungking-oriented Japanese drive into a rout. In the southwest the warning net worked so well that attacking Japanese fighter planes found no ground targets at the Hump bases.

On his return to China, General Chennault, backed by the new Trident directive for an air offensive, deployed his air forces immediately. At his direction, Casey Vincent moved his headquarters from Kunming to Kweilin on June 14. Vincent was given three squadrons of the 23rd Group totalling fifty P-40's and fifteen Mitchell B-25 bombers of the Eleventh Bombardment Squadron. Vincent's mission was to defend the Hengyang-Lingling-Kweilin line and attack Japanese-held territory in East China.

General Chennault wanted offensive strength in east China. He considered that now his hit-and-run days were over and he kept the 308th Group of heavy bombers based around Kunming, ready to blast East China Japanese-held airfields or to bombard key targets in Indo-China. Despite the weakness stemming from stateside training in the old concept that bombers did not require fighter escorts, the 308th rolled up a magnificent record over all. During one triumphant three-day operation over the Hump, the B-24's, masquerading as slow-moving, heavily-loaded transport planes, knocked eighteen unwary Japanese fighter planes out of the air and discouraged the Japanese from returning for five weeks.

On July 15 Chennault received a radio message from Casey Vincent that his forces were ready; also that the Japanese air strength in East China had risen to four hundred planes. In a few days the enemy set out to sweep the skies clean of American planes with two new type fighters, the Tojo and the Oscar Mark II.

Despite the fact that the Tojo was probably the best all-around fighter airplane in the skies over China at that time, during July, 1943, in air combat over the Hengyang-Lingling-Kweilin line, Vincent's P-40's got sixty-two confirmed kills and forty-six probables. This was too much for the Japanese and again the enemy's planes grew scarce in the skies over China. Not until August 20 did Japanese air attacks resume and this time the Japanese fighters stayed at the 30,000-foot altitude where the P-40's could not operate. Chennault ordered Vincent to attack Japanese ground bases in Canton and Hankow and by August 26 Vincent's boys had downed an additional ninety-one Jap planes confirmed and twenty-six probables. Thus the score for July, 1943, was 153 Japanese planes downed with the loss of twenty-seven Fourteenth Air Force planes.

It was this period of air fighting in 1943 that convinced the Japanese that not only could the American Air Force defeat Japanese planes and pilots in the air but that they could also prevent Japanese bombers from smashing Chinese ground targets.

With the arrival of fall, the excellent intelligence network of the Fourteenth Air Force reported that the Japanese were preparing a gigantic ground offensive. Simultaneously, with news of the beginning large-scale Jap offensive, came a dangerous slackening in the supply tonnage reaching the Fourteenth Air Force over the Hump, while Washington ignored Chennault's pleas for the new fast P-51's to replace the old and worn out P-40's which even at this late date constituted the principal part of his air force.

Chennault sent Casey Vincent back to Washington to present his pleas personally and deliver personal letters from Chennault to President Roosevelt and to

Gen. Chennault with Chief-of-Staff Brig. Gen. Glenn.
Dog is Joe. Kunming, 1944.

The Chennault laugh (rarely photographed) broke out as he looked over a chart presented by Col. John O. Neal showing what the 14th Air Force had done to the Japanese up to September 30, 1944.

Harry Hopkins. These letters explained that the supply shortages had stalled his promised objective—air superiority over China. There were no immediate results from Casey Vincent's visit.

In the fall of 1943, following additional international high level conferences, unencumbered by the presence of Claire Chennault, Stilwell was able to secure adoption of his plan for land offenses into the heavily-defended Burma jungles. In November, 1943, Stilwell left Ledo, India, to invade Burma with two Chinese divisions and three thousand American troops.

Ostensibly, Stilwell's objective was to open a land supply route into China, a route which he and a few other "experts" believed could move 100,000 tons of supplies a month. The road never delivered anything approaching that figure. In May, 1945, 6,000 tons of cargo moved over it in contrast to the 70,000 tons hauled monthly over the Hump by air.

The year 1943 in several ways opened an entirely new era of the war in China. Chinese coolies finished building the airfield at Suichwan, 250 miles east of Kweilin, which brought the Japanese-held island of Formosa within range of Chennault's fighter squadrons. On Thanksgiving Day General Vincent hurled a force of twelve B-25's escorted by P-38's and some newly arrived P-51 fighters on a bombing mission to Shinchiku, the largest Japanese training center on Formosa.

The American planes led by "Tex" Hill roared

across the Formosa Straits almost at water level to avoid the Japanese radar. The attack was a complete surprise which left forty Japanese bombers burning on the ground and six Japanese fighter planes knocked out of the air. Only one American plane was even hit.

Following the successful strike against Formosa, Chennault learned of a powerful new Japanese drive southwest of Hankow at Tungting Lake. By late November, 40,000 Japanese troops, plus half that many Koreans, with cavalry and Chinese puppet troops, had surrounded Chinese General Hsueh Yo's troops in the Lake city of Chingteh. General Hsueh Yo's ground forces fought fiercely and Chennault's Fourteenth Air Force unleashed a murderous attack which in five days killed about 15,000 Japanese troops and pushed their forces back to the positions they had held the previous December. Four American fighter squadrons and two squads of B-25 bombers made rubble of Chingteh and when new Tojo fighters rose in defense, the Fourteenth Air Force blasted them out of the air.

By New Year's Day, 1944, it was obvious to the Japanese that the only way in which they could hope to take China, including the Fourteenth Air Force's bases, would be by means of a great ground push. Only by taking and holding the entire territory of east China could the Japanese hope to protect themselves from the terrible pounding they were taking from Chennault's bombers and fighters.

At the close of 1943 the Hong Kong and Canton port areas received terrible lacings form the 308th's B-24s. The Gulf of Tonkin port and the Hainan iron-loading stations at Bakli and Samah Bay were heavily hit by B-25's flying from Yunnan bases. Additional B-25's, refueling at Suichwan, crossed the Formosa Straits to bomb Japanese tankers, freighters and radar stations. The Fourteenth's Photo Reconnaissance planes ranged over the entire enemy territory from Saigon clear to Manchuria. The Japanese were now painfully aware that the American Air Force in China was no longer defensive in nature. It was a sledge-hammer force of medium and heavy-bombing planes supported by a searing, stabbing lance of fighter planes.

The deadly American Air Force was now in position to threaten Japan's supply lifeline in the Formosa Straits and the South China Sea as well as the feeder lines to Japanese forces in the interior of China. The Flying Tigers were no longer scratching tiger cubs, merely annoying and troublesome. They were now full-grown tigers which could growl and maul and kill.

Chapter 23

Faced with the rising American air power in China, the Japanese High Command well knew that unless they could establish a land line of communications and supply along the Asian seaboard from Malaya to Manchuria, and somehow nullify the crippling Allied air strikes, they would be defeated in China. Their great and desperate land offensive, therefore, was planned as an all-out effort to aim two body blows at the Allied war effort in China. Their strategy called for a two-pronged commitment of a million and a half troops.

The southern tactical plan called for a lightning thrust by Japanese troops, based in Burma, into India in an attempt to neutralize the Assam Valley southern terminal of the Hump airlift. Simultaneously, they would launch a massive pincer operation in central and southwestern China.

The central and southwestern China campaign was divided into three stages: the first stage would be a strong ground thrust, westward from the Yellow River through Honan Province, north of Hankow, with the objective of clearing the Hankow-Peiping Railroad. This, if successful, would enable Japanese troops to move unhampered from north China into Hankow and would complete a portion of the planned Manchuria-Malaya land supply route.

The second stage would be a powerful drive south-ward out of Hankow moving down the Hankow-Canton Railway through Hunan Province.

Finally a northward push from Canton toward Chengchow was planned, thus catching the Fourteenth Air Force's bases in east China in the big north-south pincer.

If all of these moves were successful, the Japanese would have cleared a safe corridor for supplies moving from south Asia northward and for troops to move southward as needed. In addition, the danger of the Allies clearing a port for landing on the east China seaboard would have been ended.

Two things went wrong with the Japanese plans: First, their push out of Burma to cut the air supply line over the Hump failed. Secondly, Japan's conquest of the air bases in east China did not immobilize the Fourteenth Air Forces. Chennault simply retired to new bases from which he launched intensified air assaults on the enemy.

The year of 1944 was a heartbreaking, grim one for Claire Chennault. This, despite the fact that Clayton Bissell was gone. He had been replaced by a friend of Chennault's, Major General George Stratemeyer. Nevertheless, "Vinegar Joe" Stilwell was still the Theater commander and Stilwell was running into trouble with his north Burma campaign. This, in turn, meant trouble for Claire Chennault.

The General's first warnings of the Japanese land build-up came on January 27, 1944, in a field intelligence message describing preparations for enemy drives in north and south China. On February 10 he received word of heavy Japanese troop movements up the Yangtze River area toward Chengchow. The Japanese strength in the Yangtze Valley was growing from the three and a half divisions that were there in the summer of 1943 toward the fourteen divisions that were in motion in the spring of 1944.

Early in February, Chennault sent word of the Japanese build-up to General Stilwell who was moving slowly toward Myitkyina in Burma. From that time on he kept Stilwell steadily informed of the mounting danger but replies from the Theater commander were slow in arriving and offered no relief for Chennault's desperate supply situation.

Early in March the Japanese in Burma caught the British off guard and drove to within twenty miles of the Assam-Bengal railhead points. Already, the Fourteenth Air Force's supplies had been reduced to a trickle, but they now dropped forty percent as Hump air transports were diverted to rush Indian troops to the beleaguered British at Imphal.

At the end of March, Chennault, desperate now, sent a message to President Roosevelt, Generalissimo Chiang Kai-shek, General Stilwell and General Arnold in Washington: "China is in mortal danger and no preparations are possible to counter the Japanese threats unless more tonnage is delivered to the Air Force."

Stilwell replied: "Until situation at Imphal clears

up no possibility of improving your supply situation that I can see . . ."

On April 8, Chennault wrote a letter to Stilwell saying in part: "The air threat is the most serious in my experience in this theater. Disposition of the enemy's ground forces is also more threatening than at any time since Pearl Harbor."

Stilwell's reply was: "Until crisis in India passes I can see no way to improve China supply situation."

Despite intelligence reports from Stilwell's Chungking theater headquarters to the effect that the Japanese were without offensive capabilities in the Yellow River area on April 16 and 17, the same "un-offensive" Japanese troops poured three divisions of infantry and armored cars over the Yellow River and began moving at high speed across the rolling wheat fields of Honan Province.

Three days later a letter arrived from Bissell's successor, General Stratemeyer, informing Chennault that Stilwell had changed the primary designated defense mission of the Fourteenth Air Force to that of defending the newly-set-up Matterhorn project, a B-29 super-bomber group based at Chengtu in west China. The letter stated that Stilwell wanted the change "even though this may place the Fourteenth on the defensive at the expense of shipping strikes and support of Chinese ground armies."

General Chennault was stunned at what he described as "this incredible order in the face of the Japanese drive into Honan. . . . that was slicing through Chinese defenses like a knife through hot butter. Chengtu itself was in no danger. Stilwell never grasped the point that loss of east China could also mean loss of the entire China base."

The urgent warnings dispatched by Chennault to Stilwell, Generalissimo Chiang Kai-shek and others did not frighten Stilwell, intent on pursuing his hopeless jungle war in Burma, but they did impress and frighten the Generalissimo. He at once cancelled all plans for Chinese armies defending the Salween River passes to strike south into Burma according to Stilwell's plan. When this news reached Stilwell, who had been buried in the jungles for four months, the wiry little man came rushing out to argue with Generalissimo Chiang Kai-shek to reorder the Salween thrust. The Generalissimo was adamant in his refusal and in retaliation Stilwell immediately cut off every ounce of supplies coming over the Himalayas for the Chinese.

The move was effective. By May, Generalissimo Chiang Kai-shek could no longer hold out without the vital supplies. He ordered the Chinese Salween armies to move off to the south. These armies were commanded by Stilwell's deputy, Brigadier General Dorn, who had made no provisions to supply his forces as they moved south. This meant another 1,500 to 2,000 tons of monthly supplies were siphoned off the Fourteenth Air Force's already lean rations. The southern move of the Chinese Salween armies came to a quick conclusion when the armies bogged down in a stalemate with the Japanese defenders on the west bank of the Salween. During the summer this ill-fated mission wrecked two Chinese armies.

To add to the other troubles of the Fourteenth Air Force, the Matterhorn project, with its giant, gas-drinking bombers, began to eat heavily away at the precious gasoline Chennault needed for his fighters and light bombers.

Not until after the war, however, was the official conclusion reached by the U. S. Strategic Bombing survey that the China based B-29's "did not warrant diversion of the effort entailed and that the aviation gas and supplies . . . might have been more profitably allocated to expansion of tactical and shipping oper-ations of the Fourteenth Air Force." The Japanese had conquered Honan Province north of Chengchow before General Stilwell or even the American military intelligence "experts" in Chungking were to admit that an emergency existed in East China. On May 18 General Chennault sent Stilwell a final, almost frantic, warning pleading for orders, supplies and emergency procedures to defend east China. On May 24 Stilwell answered: "Until the emergency is unmistakable the decision will have to wait."

The emergency became "unmistakable" within a matter of days when the big Japanese southward push burst out of the Chengchow bulge aimed for the Kweilin-Hengyang-Lingling air bases in Hunan Prov-ince. Facing the eight divisions of the Japanese Sixth Army were ninety flyable Fourteenth Air Force airplanes with short gas rations. Orders from Washington had tied down two hundred planes for the unneeded defense of the B-29's at Chengtu and Stilwell's orders had forced Chennault to detail another 150 to the Salween drive.

The Japanese had selected the stormy, cloudy, late spring weather for their takeoff, counting on this to keep the Fourteenth Air Force bombers and fighters grounded. Facing the eight Japanese divisions were the hungry, barefoot and nearly bulletless armies of Marshal Hsueh Yo, who could do little in the face of the Japanese tidal wave. The Japanese troops flowed around the few small Chinese strong points of resistance, leaving the defenders to starve or be captured. Marshal Hsueh Yo's famous flanking tactics which had trapped and defeated the Japs on many previous occasions were useless. It was the Japanese who this time were doing the flanking.

The "unflyable" weather did indeed stop the American bombing planes for a time—but it did not stop the Fourteenth Air Force fighter planes. To "Tex" Hill's battle-scarred 23rd Fighter Group, poised at Kweilin, there was no such thing as "unflyable" weather. Heavily loaded with extra ammunition and fragmentation bombs, the fighters sloshed off through mud and rain and fog and roared in low under 300- and 400-foot fog ceilings to attack the Japanese. The stabbing, low-level attacks slaughtered columns of 200 to 2,000 Japanese soldiers at a time. As a part of the Japanese drive floated across Tungting Lake and up the Siang River in sampans and other craft, the American fighters strafed and bombed them, leaving the wreckage of boats and sampans and dead bodies stalling traffic on the lake and the river.

Lightning P-38's of the Fourteenth Air Force, carrying twenty-millimeter cannons in their noses, struck the east flank and time and again stalled the main supply line for the Japanese drive over a single-lane highway packed with heavily loaded trucks. But with a limited number of planes available and no ground support, the Fourteenth Air Force could not possibly halt the big enemy offensive. In June General Stilwell came out of his Burma jungle for two or three days during which he visited Kunming, announced that nothing could be done to halt the Japanese offensive in East China and discussed the crises for a half-hour with Chennault. To Chennault's plea that every military resource available in the CBI theater be brought to bear immediately to halt the Japanese threat Stilwell returned an uncompromising "No." Chennault then asked for three minimum moves: one, immediate increase of the Fourteenth Air Force Hump supply priority to 11,000 tons a month to which General Stilwell agreed. However, this could not take effect at the fighting front for sixty days.

To Chennault's second request, emergency action including a sharp increase in fuel allocation for the Fourteenth's land supply line running from Hump

Yunnan terminals through the mountains to the east China front, Stilwell's answer was a firm "No." He gave an affirmative to Chennault's third request that he be permitted to launch a one-hundred-plane B-29 mission to knock out Chengchow, a Japanese strong point. Stilwell's affirmative response, however, actually meant "no" since he merely forwarded Chennault's request to Washington with a routine endorsement. This was not enough to obtain affirmative Pentagon action and Stilwell knew it. The Washington approval did not come for five months which was a month after east China had been completely lost.

One of General Chennault's deepest regrets was the loss of Hengyang to the Japanese, which he could have prevented had he been allowed to do so. The story of Hengyang is an epic one, although it got little attention in the world press, with the events in Europe making the big headlines. Furthermore, most of the Far East reporters were with Stilwell in Burma.

The Japanese Sixth Army moved swiftly past Chengchow to within ten minutes flying time from the Fourteenth Hengyang air field still occupied by the stubborn "Tex" Hill and his Twenty-Third Fighter Group. "Tex" gambled for three days on bad weather holding down the Japanese Air Force, during which time they strafed the advancing columns with devastating effect. Finally, on June 26, with the Japanese only twenty miles away, the Americans burned and destroyed their Hengyang base and retired to

Lingling, ninety miles to the south from which they kept on harassing.

The Japanese ground forces arrived to face the biggest single obstacle of their east China campaign: the heavily dug in Chinese Tenth Army under the command of General Fong Hsien Chien, one of Marshal Hsueh Yo's best commanders. Fong was cut off from reinforcements but he had ten thousand veteran troops, three French .75 field pieces, machine guns and mortars and handmade Chinese rifles for almost every other soldier. Faced with this stubborn well-dug-in force, the Japanese ground blitz was halted, giving the Fourteenth Air Force a chance to blast them—a chance which the Fourteenth did not miss. All of the Japanese supply avenues leading to the Hengyang siege took a terrible lacing of fragmentation bombs and P-38 cannon assaults.

Early in July, 1944, the weather broke and the Japanese Oscars and Tojos ventured out of hiding— to lose one-hundred-twenty airplanes in East China skies and the heart of the enemy bomber force— ninety airplanes—on the ground. Japanese troops from the besiegers' lines were captured on food-foraging expeditions through the countryside. The supply lines behind them were falling. Some troop units were still fighting on two hundred rounds of ammunition issued at the outset of their drive south from Changsha. Although on July 8, the Japanese pressure on Hengyang relaxed, the Japanese made a final effort to renew their pressure, knowing that this was their big chance. By mid-July the enemy was back in siege action with 40,000 fresh troops, heavy artillery and tanks. By this time, a half-million men were engaged in the mightly Japanese land offensive.

The renewed Japanese pressure brought a final time of crisis for General Fong's embattled men in Hengyang. The continued refusal of General Stilwell to help made Chennault feel that Stilwell was determined to withhold help until and unless he was given command of all Chinese armies. General Chennault pleaded with the CBI commander to help the brave holdouts in Hengyang but Stilwell refused. Finally, Chennault sent the Fourteenth Air Force's own B-25's and C-47's to air drop rice, medical supplies and ammunition to the beleagured Chinese troops. He also sent a half dozen additional pleas to General Stilwell and received straight refusals. Chennault's final desperate plea for five hundred tons to be dropped to the brave, besieged troops, met with refusal.

Finally, Chennault realized that the end was approaching for Hengyang. But even he did not anticipate a gasoline shortage that would cut off the last vestige of support for the Chinese armies. From July 17 until July 23 every airplane under Chennault's command was grounded for lack of gasoline. Five days before the end of July fuel began to trickle back into the Fourteenth's supply line but it was too late. On August 8 in a powerful artillery infantry and armored sweep the Japanese moved into Hengyang. The fate of East China was sealed.

For the remainder of the summer and until mid-November the Fourteenth Air Force fought with increasing vigor as gasoline supplies picked up, and the big Japanese push, now off-balance and off schedule, never regained its early enormous momentum. Nevertheless, it moved doggedly on through East China and the remaining advanced air bases of the Fourteenth Air Force fell one by one. Finally Liuchow, the last of the East China Fourteenth Air Force bases gave up on November 7. Now the conquest of East China by the Japanese was complete.

"Both the Japanese and the U. S. Joint Chiefs of Staff, prompted by Stilwell's dire predictions, thought the smoke of Liuchow's burning hostels and blown runways meant the end of the Fourteenth Air Force in China," Chennault wrote. "Both were in for a big surprise."

Part **4** *Fire in the Autumn*

"We have never come at the true and
best benefit of any genius so long as we
believe him an original force. In the moment when he ceases to help us as a cause,
he begins to help us more as an effect."

RALPH WALDO EMERSON (1803-82)
"USE OF GREAT MEN"

Chapter 24

My husband always thought it the height of irony that Lt. General Joseph Warren "Vinegar Joe" Stilwell, after three determined years of trying to build a Chinese military empire under his supreme command, finally brought the structure he had so carefully and ruthlessly erected crashing down upon his head by one act of pique.

In the autumn of 1944, a special American mission, headed by Major General Patrick J. Hurley and the former U. S. War Production Board, Donald Nelson, conducted a series of delicate negotiations in Chungking to win Chiang Kai-shek's despairing consent to the proposed supreme Stilwell command of all Chinese forces. The Americans found the Chinese Generalissimo so dejected over the collapsing East front in China that he was willing to give up almost anything, including full command of his armies, if it would secure fast expanded American aid. Otherwise, the Generalissimo knew, China faced total military defeat and economic ruin.

Agreement on all important points, including the Stilwell command, was reached by mid-September. Only details needed to be ironed out in further meetings between the Americans and the Chinese head of Government. At this point a strange message bearing the radioed signature of President Roosevelt arrived at Chungking CBI headquarters for delivery to Chiang Kai-shek.

According to General Chennault, one of the two or three Americans who saw a copy of that message said it sounded like a communication from Adolf Hitler to the puppet head of a conquered satellite nation. Roosevelt, in violent terms, blamed the Generalissimo for China's present plight and presented an ultimatum to appoint Stilwell as Chinese commander. The tone of the message was entirely foreign to the President's usual manner toward the Generalissimo. Some strongly suspected Stilwell had written the message himself, sent it "eyes alone" to Washington, where the War Department had persuaded Roosevelt to sign it.

Hurley and Nelson were staggered when they heard about the message and pleaded with General Stilwell not to deliver it. They thought they had won his concurrence but on September 21 General Stilwell strode into the Huang Shan conferences and read Generalissimo Chiang Kai-shek the Roosevelt message. In his own published papers, Stilwell stated that he took this action to "break the peanut's face." The Generalissimo listened to the recital in silence and let Stilwell leave without saying a word. He was pale, and the big vein in his forehead was pulsing with suppressed anger as his visitor left.

The drama-packed scene in Chiang Kai-shek's villa blasted General Stilwell out of China. The Generalissimo notified the American mission that he considered the Roosevelt message a flat challenge to the sovereignty of China. He said that Stilwell must go if it meant China would never get another rifle bullet from America.

Negotiations on the Sino-American pact containing provisions for an American overall command in China deadlocked immediately. They remained deadlocked until the United States agreed to bring General Wedemeyer up from Mountbatten's headquarters in Kandy, Ceylon to take the job. They were then quickly signed, and the War Department radioed Joe Stilwell to come home.

The tragic failure of General Stilwell in China was mourned by many of the press, and the world, as the defeat of a simple soldier by oriental complicity and guile. In my husband's opinion, and in mine, it was nothing of the sort. General Stilwell's departure removed from the Far East combat arena a commander whose arbitrary orders withheld all forms of help from the ally, China, when that ally was being beaten to its knees and overrun by the enemy. It opened the way for the United States Fourteenth Air Force under Major General Claire Chennault to rescue China from World War II conquest and ruin.

My husband was not sorry to see Stilwell go, carrying with him out of China the curious mixture of pride, prejudice, misunderstanding and misdirected determination that poisoned Chinese-American relationships for two critical years and hamstrung effective Allied operations in Asia.

The general felt that in the gulf between Stilwell's simplicity and the intricacies of his position as the top-ranking American in CBI that his troubles began. During this struggle with problems he only vaguely understood, there fermented the increasing bitterness that marked Stilwell's final year as CBI theater commander.

"Not many lifelong professional soldiers do well in diplomatic assignments," the General once told me. "Eisenhower and Wedemeyer were the exceptions, Stilwell the rule."

Chapter 25

According to legend, every year the Phoenix—an immortal bird in Egyptian mythology—was consumed by fire and immediately resurrected, rising young and strong in its own ashes. To scholars and historians, the similarity between the legendary Phoenix and the modern U. S. Fourteenth Air Force under my husband, General Chennault, will, I am sure, be inescapable.

Four days after the Japanese captured the last of the East China American bases—Liuchow—Chinese and American fighters from Chihkiang, the Fourteenth's key base for air guerrilla operations behind the Japanese lines, struck back. They zoomed in on Hengyang, the big, newly occupied base one hundred miles to the north, and shot down and burned on the ground an entire unit of thirty Jap fighters and a dozen bombers. The Japs never attempted to use Hengyang for sustained operations again.

The pattern of heavy and effective Fourteenth Air Force onslaught continued through December. Free of "Vinegar Joe" Stilwell's restrictive control, no longer tied down all over China by ground-support assigments, and with General Chennault and the CBI Theater Command working hand-in-glove, the American fliers forged a terrible weapon. Dating from mid-November, 1944, in China, not a Japanese airplane, troop unit, supply warehouse, staging base, truck convoy, locomotive, or a boat on the maze of Chinese waterways or even offshore, was safe any longer. Once unchained, the Fourteenth fighters and bombers taught Japan the hard way the lesson General Chennault eternally preached—without strong airpower, in modern warfare no nation can long survive.

The powerful reach of the 14th extended beyond China's borders far out into the Formosa Straits and the South China Sea. A striking demonstration of the Fourteenth's strategic role from its East China bases came on October 16 after Navy carrier planes and China-based B-29's had pounded Formosan ports and airfields for three days. Nearly 200,000 tons of enemy shipping scuttled across the South China Sea from Formosan ports to seek refuge in Hong Kong's spacious harbor. They had hardly dropped anchor when the Fourteenth struck them with all its might.

The effect was devastating. The Americans sank eight freighters and damaged eleven with 80,000 tons of shipping out of action and major damage to one of Japan's largest repair facilities.

Another demonstration of the Fourteenth's strategic role came during the Second Battle of the Philippine Sea, considered by the Navy the decisive sea fight of the war. During this critical period only China-based Liberators of the Fourteenth could provide the Navy with reconnaissance on its blind western flank in the South China Sea. Carrying extra gas loads for greater range, Liberators flew Navy-specified patrols over the fleet's blind spots. It was a Fourteenth Air Force Liberator that alerted the Navy to the Japanese carrier task-force steaming south from the Pescadores to attack the defenders of the Leyte beachhead. The Fourteenth Air Force Liberators earned a "well done" from Admirals Nimitz and Halsey for their work in locating retiring units of the Japanese fleet to permit submarine strikes along the line of retreat. During the months while East China was holding out, Liberators mined major Japanese harbors from Shanghai to Saigon and sank a quarter of a million tons of merchant shipping, two enemy cruisers, and four destroyers. This also was part of the enormous price the enemy paid for East China.

Easy as they looked, the amazing series of crushing blows dealt the Japanese demanded the kind of chess-like war strategy and tactics General Chennault understood so well and exercised so effectively. With a mighty assist from Chinese coolies, building airfields almost literally in a matter of hours, he swung his entire 750-miles-long east-west line of offensive air bases to create an equally long north-south axis, parallelling Japanese forces. The new line was topped in the north with a triangle of bases in Shensi Province, and dropped almost straight south to Poseh, in the Province of Kwangsi.

The new team running the new, separate China Theater—Lieutenant General Al Wedemeyer and Major General Claire Chennault—was working like a charm. The dark war picture in China brightened daily to optimism and firm Sino-American unity. This had never been achieved before, in thirty grim months of staggering Chinese losses and defeats on the ground, of countless Chennault air rescue strikes cancelled for lack of gasoline, and of internal war operations command disputes that brought China to the verge of utter ruin.

General Wedemeyer began the job which in six months would end Chinese distrust and suspicion of her ally, the United States. He would win back the confidence of Chiang Kai-shek and other Chinese leaders lost by Stilwell. He would organize a sound Sino-American military program in China, and train and arm Chinese troops to carry it out. Finally, and most importantly, he would properly employ and supply the Fourteenth Air Force to whip the Japanese so fast and so badly that heavy ground operations would never be needed.

"Wedemeyer," wrote General Chennault, "is a man of great personal integrity and studied fairness in his dealings with others. He found it possible to deal effectively with the Generalissimo and other Chinese leaders on a frank yet dignified basis without rising to truculence or sinking to subservience. As a result he found his advice accepted, his plans carried out, and his opinions valued . . .

"With the passing of Stilwell from the China scene it was possible to begin an effective joint Sino-American war effort even though it was just two years late . . ."

General Wedemeyer fully realized the strategic value of the Fourteenth Air Force's lashing blows along the 2,300-mile Japanese front in East China. He was the Fourteenth's most vigorous champion before the high court of military powers running the war. As the Wedemeyer-Chennault team got into action, the Fourteenth was given top priority for Hump supplies, even when other planned activities had to be curtailed to keep the Chennault forces at operating maximum. Even this support by Wedemeyer gave the Fourteenth nothing like all the supplies needed, but it maintained steady operations.

When General Chennault brought up again his six-month-old plan to flatten Hankow, the biggest base and real keystone of Japanese strength in China, he now received enthusiastic backing at Theater headquarters. It was too late to halt the Japanese East China land offensive—as might have been done earlier—but if Hankow was neutralized it would still be a mortal blow at Japanese strength. Wedemeyer quickly won Pentagon permission to use one hundred of the B-29's based at Chengtu for a spearhead.

General Chennault and General Curtis LeMay, recently transferred from the bombardment war in Europe to command the China-based B-29's, worked out an agreement for the attack plan for the bombing of Hankow.

Shortly before noon on December 18, seventy-seven

B-29's opened the attack on Hankow. They roared over in seven waves ten minutes apart. By the time the first thirty-five Superforts had dumped their incendiaries, Hankow was completely obscured by a heavy blanket of smoke.

These December 18 raids destroyed Hankow as a major base for the Japanese army and air force in Central China. For three days, fires burned redly, gutting the docks, warehouse areas and much of the foreign quarter of the city.

Late in December and in early January came more good news and greater strength for the Fourteenth. The long-promised replacements of fresh pilots and P-51C Mustang fighters arrived. These airplanes—one hundred fifty miles-an-hour faster than the old P-40's and in general flown by pilots eager to fight—grew so aggresive that missions of four to eight Mustangs attacked enemy formations numbering between thirty and forty airplanes. The Japs used improved Tojos and Oscars, with a few newer planes —the Franks, Jacks and liquid-cooled Tonies—but they couldn't match the Mustangs and American pilots.

The squadrons of Herbst and McComas practically cleaned out enemy air strength at Canton, Hong Kong, and the Yangtze River fields from Hankow to Nanking, in the next sixty days. On one dawn attack, they caught enemy pilots at breakfast in lighted barracks while mechanics out on the field warmed up airplanes for a big raid—and killed forty pilots and one hundred mechanics. In their final strike at Canton, Herbst led sixteen Mustangs over the city and circled lazily as the Japs frantically scrambled up to meet them. Thirteen of the Japs went down in flames and the Mustangs flew down to treetop level and used up the rest of their ammunition field-strafing.

December's record of two hundred forty-one enemy planes shot down by the Fourteenth was shattered in January, with a new record of three hundred thirty-four. Suddenly, Japanese airplanes began to get scarce. The shoot-downs dropped to forty-seven in March, with the Fourteenth roving all over China, and in April American airplanes met only three Japanese in the air. From May 15 until July 1, not a single enemy airplane was sighted in flight. In the six months between November 15, 1944, and May 15, 1945, the Fourteenth had accounted for 1,634 enemy airplanes, with the loss of only sixteen American planes in air combat.

The Japanese Air Force in China was annihilated.

Chapter 26

During the winter of 1944-45, the Fourteenth Air Force applied the type of air pressure on the Japanese supply lines that Chennault had hoped to apply a year earlier when the Japanese armies were gathering strength for the great spring offensive of 1944. At that time, however, half of his fighter strength had been immobilized in the defense of the Chengtu B-29 air bases and the remaining forces at his disopsal were eking out a bare existence on the short end of the supply line.

The long campaign against the Yangtze River shipping continued. Liberators methodically mined the river and reconnaissance and fighter sweeps were continually reporting sighting ships sunk or burning in areas where no air attacks had been carried out for days. Such Japanese casualties were attributed to the contact, sonic and magnetic mines which had so liberally been sown.

But the main force of the Fourteenth Air offensive was thrown against the railroad. Throughout an enormous area roughly equaling a territory stretching from Miami to Montreal and from Washington, D. C., to Kansas City, Missouri, nothing that moved on China's roads or railroads was safe from the air attacks of the Fourteenth's fighters and bombers.

By March, 1945, the transportation attacks were

beginning to really hurt the enemy. Japanese supplies on key lines had dwindled between forty and seventy-five percent. Japanese troop movements from Hankow to Peiping that had taken a week in 1944 now required three months. Since January of 1945 the Fourteenth Air Force had wrecked 2,500 locomotives and 5,000 railroad cars, had smashed three hundred seventy-three bridges and had destroyed two thousand trucks.

By the end of March, 1945, Japanese armies south of Hankow were receiving less than half the supplies they needed for bare subsistence. After the war Lieutenant General Takahashi, commander of the Japanese Central China Expeditionary force, said that he received only half of his armies' minimum needs during May because of American air attacks.

By the end of May hunger drove the enemy northward, harassed along every mile of their way by Fourteenth Air Force fighters and medium bombers. Disease helped thin the ranks of the fleeing enemy. The hot early summer weather of south China brought malaria, cholera and typhoid fever to the undernourished and exhausted survivors of American air attacks. For the first time in the Sino-Japanese war the enemy was forced to leave behind large numbers of unburied dead.

With the end of Japanese effective resistance in China came also the final days of my husband's tenure as American Air Forces commander in China. Stung and embittered by his ouster from China, Stilwell had

returned to Washington to pour his woes into the
attentive ears of General George Marshall, blaming
most of his failure upon General Chennault. Marshall
believed Stilwell. He told General Wedemeyer that
Chennault had been disloyal to Stilwell, that Chennault had failed completely in East China, and that
he would never approve another promotion or decoration for him.

Wedemeyer told Chennault he had seen nothing to
support Marshall's contention during the time he and
Chennault had worked together, but that Marshall
had left him no alternative but to ease Chennault out.
Chennault had always liked Wedemeyer, had been
able to work smoothly with him and trusted him completely. He told Wedemeyer that if Marshall's charges
were true he deserved a courtmartial and twice declared that he would welcome such a test. General
Wedemeyer persuaded my husband that because the
entire affair was below the surface and unofficial the
only course was to forget it.

In April, 1945, General Wedemeyer arrived back
in China following a conference in Washington to
which he had been called by General Marshall. Wedemeyer now had no choice but to carry out his orders
to ease General Chennault out of China. He delayed,
however, putting the plan into effect until July 6 because he believed he could not dispense with my husband's services any earlier than that. Under the plan
forced upon Wedemeyer during his visit to Washington the Fourteenth Air Force was to be reduced to the

Gen. Chennault is honor guest at a farewell dinner given by Generalissimo Chiang Kai-shek, on his departure for the U.S. after relinquishing command of the 14th U.S. Air Force. To the Generalissimo's right is U.S. Ambassador Patrick J. Hurley. Facing them is Lt. Gen. Albert C. Wedemeyer, commander of U.S. armed forces in China-Burma-India. To Gen. Chennault's left is China's wartime foreign minister, Dr. Wong Shih-Chih.

Maj. Gen. Claire L. Chennault, U.S.A. (Ret.), receiving the Navy Distinguished Service Medal from Admiral Charles M. Cooke, Jr., Commander Naval Forces Western Pacific, in Shanghai. Gen. Chennault then headed the Civil Air Transport Company, largest commercial air freight concern in China. December 9, 1947.

size of an air wing. This meant that, in effect, General Chennault would be replacing one of his own wing commanders. From Calcutta, General George Stratemeyer would move to Chungking to set up Army Air Force headquarters, China Theater, and serve as air adviser to Wedemeyer. Stratemeyer would command all air forces in China, including the Chinese Air Force. Dearly though my husband wished to remain in China, he knew that for the second time in his career he would have to resign.

On July 8, 1945, exactly eight years from the day that he had first offered his services to China, General Chennault requested release from active duty and retirement from the Army. Again, he gave ill health as his official reason. The Chinese understood this perfectly. It is a device they too use in similar situations.

Here again was one of the many bitter ironies that studded Claire Chennault's career. Once more he had struggled and fought and had proved all of his early theories of aviation tactics. He had achieved a record unequalled in air annals. Once again the military brass had not recognized or appreciated. Plaudits and acclaim would come later from his own countrymen—not from Stilwell or men like him but from others who, after the tumult and the shouting had died, would finally see matters in true perspective.

The Chinese did not wait until after the war to register their acclaim. During General Chennault's farewell swing through China, during which he visited the main bases of the Fourteenth Air Force—Teishiyi, Sian, Chengtu, Luliang and Kunming—he also stopped at Chungking where, as I mentioned many chapters earlier, he received the greatest acclaim accorded any "foreigner" in the history of China. In the evening in Chungking, following that great public daytime tribute, Generalissimo Chiang Kai-shek decorated General Chennault with the Order of the White Sun and the Blue Sky. He was the first "foreigner" ever to receive such an honor. On the same occasion, General Wedemeyer pinned a second Oak Leaf Cluster to the General's Distinguished Service Medal.

On August 8, after farewell parties in Kunming, the General's staff C-47 transport plane rolled down the runway carrying "Chennote Chiang Chun" on the first leg of his long air voyage to the United States. That trip would begin with the hazardous flight over the Hump with its capricious winds and treacherous weather.

As he left China one thought sustained him. Pentagon politics had seen to it that to save the face of General Stilwell, military and diplomatic failure, Chennault would not be in on the finish of Japan to get credit for what he had done. But thanks to Wedemeyer's and Stratemeyer's honesty he had finished his job. There was no longer a Japanese air force in China and without air cover what was left of a Japanese land army and a Japanese shipping supply line was in cowering, demoralized rout. Now the enemy was as desperate under the Fourteenth's unopposed bombs and machine guns as the Chinese cities had been under the unopposed Japanese bombers before the AVG arrived. For few men in history had the wheel so dramatically come full circle.

But as the General's C-47 winged west over the towering Himalayas, neither he nor we in Kunming knew how dramatically complete was his country's triumph. The war with Japan was over!

For on that very day, August 8, 1945, the world's first atom bomb fell on Hiroshima. And a few days later as General Chennault flew west past India, over the Nile Delta on the way from Tel Aviv to Athens, the plane radio of his C-47 brought the news—Japan had formally surrendered.

But, I remember wondering, with Roosevelt dead, would Claire Chennault live long enough to get credit in his lifetime for what he had done?

He would. Thirteen years later, when he was buried in Arlington, with the almost-posthumous third star of a Lieutenant General on his shoulder, there walked behind his caisson to acknowledge their peer, every great air general of the Pacific War—Nathan Twining, Carl Spaatz, Thomas D. White, Albert C. Wedemeyer, George Kenney, "Rosy" O'Donnell, Curtis LeMay (now Air Force Chief of Staff) and Bedell Smith representing President Eisenhower. On his breast were the Distinguished Service Medal with oak leaf cluster, Distinguished Flying Cross, Legion of Merit, Air Medal, Chinese Order of Celestial Banner,

3rd class, Order of the Blue Sky and White Sun, Commander—Order of the British Empire, all honestly earned, over and over again, by sweat, blood and tears.

On September 2, 1945, three weeks after he left Kunming, his old champion, Merian Cooper, formerly Chief-of-Staff of the China Air Task Force, then with General Kenney's Fifth Air Force stood with General MacArthur and General Kenney on the deck of the battleship "Missouri" in Tokyo Bay as the Japanese Empire surrendered.

MacArthur asked a question. "Where," he said, "is Chennault?"

Chapter 27

Like the General, the Flying Tigers came home from China and are now organizations only in their Association whose extraordinary vitality is proof of their belief that beyond other men in the war they shared an extraordinary experience. My story should therefore end here. But although the General's later career is properly a whole new story in itself, I think a short resumé of how he finished life sheds a backward light on his character in the Flying Tigers.

Now 52 years old, the General, still convinced that in the future of China lay the peace of the West, came back to start a new career in China. Fêted in the U. S., he was offered enthusiastic backing for public office. As a famous airman he was offered high salaries, executive positions in airlines. However, what had made the General risk everything to achieve impossibilities in the war had been his passionate belief, for which he had sacrificed promotion and pay, that the future of China would determine the peace of the U. S. and at any cost he followed this conviction to the bitter end.

On New Year's Day in 1945 he was back in Shanghai to see what he could do to repair the devastation of communications by which his own 14th Air Force, while driving out the Japs, had reduced China to disease and starvation. Wrecked railroads, wrecked river boats, downed bridges, bomb-blasted highways made it impossible for food to move from farm to town or for relief food and epidemic medicine to move out of port warehouses. UNRRA relief spoiled on docks or was pilfered for the black market. Away from the docks in the interior of China thousands were eating tree bark and clay just to keep their stomachs feeling full.

Airman Chennault had believed in the Himalayan airlift before anyone else. Chennault realized that time was all important in China not only for the starving thousands but for the stability of the war-weary government. He therefore proposed an air freight line operated for UNRRA to distribute relief supplies to the back country. The local UNRRA chief—Ralph Olmstead, now an executive of Morrison-Knudsen Company, saw the possibilities. All other UNRRA officials, until the proposals finally got up to the desk of Fiorello LaGuardia, and top UNRRA chief, himself an old airman, were appalled at the difficulties. Two commercial airlines already operating in China but without capacity to carry relief supplies themselves opposed the idea vigorously.

At this point the General sent for the "Washington Squadron" and two of its members came and stayed. The first was the famous Whiting Willauer, later to be Ambassador to Honduras and Costa Rica, one of the leaders in the deposing of Guatemalan Communist President Arbenz, and one of the first to detect and warn about Cuban Communist Castro. Willauer, a brilliant Harvard Law School lawyer from Boston, had been working in the Civil Aeronautics Administration in Washington when Tom Corcoran put him into China Defense Supplies. With the 14th he had been in China on the educating task of flying supplies over the Hump into the forward bases hundreds of miles further East and then by any kind of surface transportation available, even coolies rolling gasoline drums. Later he had come back to Shanghai as chief of the U. S. Foreign Economic Administration for all Asia not occupied by the military forces. He was an imaginative lawyer, an excellent administrator who knew U. S. airline methods and was himself a multi-engine pilot, physically the bravest of the brave whom men adoringly followed. When Chennault mentioned his airline project to Willauer in Shanghai, Willauer wanting to do something more effective than the sterile stalemate of his government job, resigned and joined Chennault as his partner.

With first funds from the "Washington Squadron," with yeomen help from their fellow airman, Fiorello LaGuardia, who overruled the intermediate echelons of UNRRA and upheld Olmstead, the partners got a contract from UNRRA to haul relief supplies which let them buy 25 old C-47 cargo planes from the surplus dump in Hawaii. A third of the planes were to be "cannibalized" for spare parts.

With this beaten-up equipment and with pilots and mechanics from men in the AVG and the 14th, from Marine Aviation and other American outfits who chose to stay in the Far East, they started. The first flight was made in late January, 1947, transporting UNRRA supplies from Shanghai to Canton. During this year Chennault and Willauer concentrated almost entirely on hauling relief food and medical supplies brought to China by UNRRA into the otherwise inaccessible back areas of China which Chennault knew as no other airman in the world.

The operation was so successful that toward the end of 1947 at the expiration of the UNRRA contract, the Chinese Government encouraged them to break out on their own with half Chinese partners, to haul commercial cargoes inbound to balance relief cargoes outbound. Within another year they were the largest freight line in the world, covering a territory from Mukden to Lanchow to Canton, equivalent in American terms to an area bounded by Boston and Denver and New Orleans.

At this point another of the "Washington Squadron," James Brennan, already in China as the American secretary to Premier T. V. Soong, resigned his job and joined Chennault. He became the Treasurer of the airline, with Willauer as Executive Vice-President and Chennault as President. Brennan was to command the last flight out of Canton on the Chinese Mainland in the final evacuation to Hong Kong. But over the years he had especially acquired a facility for understanding and working with the complications of Chinese politics and business. This was eventually to leave him in charge of working out the final "miracle" of Chennault's resistance to Chinese Communism—Willauer's "legal kidnapping" of the 80 U. S. air freight planes which the Communists had hoped to acquire on their recognition by Britain and with which they had intended to mount an aerial assault on Formosa. This was a famous series of lawsuits in which Chennault's adviser was no one less than Roscoe Pound, former Dean of the Harvard Law School and once the Chinese Government's adviser on legal reform.

The Chennault-Willauer airline, Civil Air Transport, was soon shortened to CAT, as it is known today.* It literally carried anything anywhere. In early days people often shared accommodations with cattle, sheep and pigs. No one seemed to mind although a pilot occasionally looked behind the cockpit into the velvety eyes of a cow thoughtfully surveying the cloud banks. On many occasions pilots and ground personnel were quartered in tents, pilots doubled as passenger agents weighing freight and collecting fares; nor was the pay princely. But the adventurous, hard-working and fanatically loyal working staff of CAT stuck with the airline through every hardship.

There was never any question about CAT's competence. Staffed with many ex-AVG and 14th Air Force and other military pilots, there was a military appearance to CAT. Its bucket-seat planes, and the

*CAT: President—Hugh Grundy; Chairman—George A. Doole, Jr.

maintenance lessons its personnel had learned in the war soon gave it a safety record and a capacity to fly round the clock in all weather; it quickly developed an unsurpassed safety record due in no small measure to Chennault's intimate knowledge of China's weather and terrain. Nothing else flying in China could begin to match it although it operated with generally over-loaded planes in some of the worst weather in the world with no navigational ground aids but its own.

Soon, however, Chennault was again at war. The same war-weariness with which England dropped Churchill infected China as well as the rest of the world. In addition to being war-weary, China was so devastated that the government had no resources except U. S. aid with which to fight new enemies. Breaking their promises to Roosevelt at Yalta to help the Nationalist Government in its post-war reconstruction, the Russians backed a take-over by the Chinese Communists who during the whole war had been waiting for their chance to overthrow the war government. Striking on the western flank of the far flung Nationalist armies which had been transported by the U. S. Navy to the extreme north to defend Manchuria, the Communist menace began to strike down one isolated key northern city after another.

As the Communist threat gathered momentum in North China, air transportation over a country devastated of land communication became vital. To meet the need CAT expanded rapidly. Its unarmed planes were attacked furiously by the Communists. It became a "combat airline." As *Time* magazine later described it, it was "the most shot at airline in the world." When other airlines flinched, almost single-handedly CAT maintained the vital aerial transportation system, flying in or dropping not only munitions to armies but food and medicine to thousands of starving, sick and besieged people. While CAT flew in supplies to continue the fighting, it flew out precious machinery, capital, treasures, and key personnel which it kept moving ahead of the Communist onslaught. When the final evacuation of the Chinese Nationalists to their island bastion on Formosa became imminent, it was CAT that made possible an incredible lift of men and equipment.

For a full year CAT and Chennault were indispensable in delaying the total enslavement of the anti-Communist Mainland Chinese. Probably only Claire Chennault would have believed it possible to accomplish this with an unarmed commercial freight airline which couldn't fire back on the advancing Chinese Communist armies—troops armed with Russian supplies at a time when U. S. aid hesitated and hoped for appeasement.

CAT, perfecting the air drop techniques of the war, became expert in flying supplies over siege lines the Communists had set around prosperous cities and army garrisons. They even flew into and out of walled cities.

CAT was really a prototype of the Berlin airlift

which was later commanded by General Curtis LeMay who had been with Chennault in China. When one city, Chengchow in North China, was cut off, CAT flew in cotton to keep its mills at work. When whole Nationalist armies in Manchuria, transported north by the U. S. Navy, were cut off, CAT staged a gigantic airlift totalling 50 flights a day. In one 24-hour period it transported into the Manchurian trap a record of 219,000 tons of military and civilian cargo.

One of CAT's finest hours was when it enabled one-half million civilians and soldiers in the Pittsburgh of China, Taiyuan, to hold out for nine months although completely surrounded. As the siege lines tightened, 15 air strips had to be constructed and used as they were in turn destroyed by Communist artillery fire. Under that fire CAT kept landing ammunition and supplies, also dropping rice in double bags for the civilian population. (An inner tight bag would split upon ground impact but a loose outer bay would hold.) These operations were conducted not only under fire but over greater distances than those of the Berlin airlift and when a city could not finally be held, thousands of troops and civilians were evacuated by CAT planes to fall back and fight again.

As the AVG and CATF and the 14th had to do when the Jap armies overran their bases, CAT shifted its bases from field to field, west and south, as the Communists advanced and American aid was inde-

cisive. CAT headquarters at Shanghai were succes-
sively abandoned for Canton, for Kunming, for
Hainan Island, finally for Formosa. This created a
problem in which the CAT resourcefulness was at its
best. The jugular of the airline was its maintenance
workshops which could not be moved quickly from
field to field. Willauer finally hit upon establishing
the machine shops on a floating base, a war surplus
LST (landing ship tank) towing a barge. Headquarters fields were hereafter always on the coast and
when any headquarters was in danger, the maintenance base sailed away to a new one. This floating
base was never captured nor was a single plane lost
until the over-confident crew of one, ignoring orders,
stayed overnight near the old AVG base in Kunming.

Under such incredible conditions only the inspiration of a leader like Chennault could have held a
civilian group together; but the spirit of the brave
and intrepid personnel of CAT was also incredible.
There was, for instance, a day in 1950 when Chinese
inflation temporarily bankrupted the airline. Chennault called everyone together at Hong Kong to tell
them that salaries would have to be cut in half and
that even this reduced amount could not be promised
in the foreseeable future. He gave the employees his
sincere advice to quit and find other jobs. They
merely pulled in their belts, pledged their continued
loyalty and went back to work.

CAT not only fought the Communist war in China;
it was first into the breach to help MacArthur when

the Communists attacked in Korea. It fought in Vietnam as well, stepping in when the French could no longer supply their foreign legion at Dien Bien Phu, which actually did not fall from assault but from lack of supplies. In the last rush the defenders, without a round of ammunition, were wrestled down by the Communists. For a month—until the last day—the only line of supply was the CAT air-drop. And the morning after the crash of the last CAT plane that could get in, with "Earthquake" McGoon piloting it and dying, the strong point fell.

The General is dead, Whiting Willauer is dead, James Brennan has come home to the United States and many a famous pilot has left. But CAT still flies— now a plush airline with jet planes you may yourself have ridden—from Seoul to Tokyo to Okinawa to Formosa to Hong Kong to Bangkok, flying Free China's flag in defiance of the barbarian giant on the Communist mainland. And in Laos and South Vietnam not CAT but many an old CAT pilot is still air-dropping supplies to anti-Communist defenders carrying Chennault's anti-Communist fight beyond the grave.

Even after the Free China Government and CAT were driven back to Formosa, the General, Willauer and Brennan with the help of Dean Pound, and the "Washington Squadron" together with General William Donovan performed one last anti-Communist "miracle.'

When CAT had started, there had been two

other airlines on the mainland of China owned by the Nationalist Government. Between them they had nearly 100 modern planes—gifts from the U. S.— much bigger and faster than CAT's little battle-worn fleet and by far the best non-military air fleet in the Far East. In the days of despair on the Mainland, Communist agents with Hong Kong merchants conspiring with them, persuaded the managers of these airlines to defect and fly all the planes to Hong Kong to await British recognition of Communist China. The idea was that once on British soil, transfer of title to the whole fleet would come to the Communist Government when the British Government recognized Communist China. American pilots in the defecting lines tipped off Chennault and Willauer. Chennault well knew that if he were in charge of Communist air power, he could with such a fleet stage an airborne assault on unconsolidated Formosa that might even take the island. Through the legal ingenuity of Willauer, Chennault and Willauer personally acquired title to the whole fleet before the British recognition of Communist China took place, claiming the planes as American-owned. For five years they fought a legal battle against the Hong Kong merchants who sympathized with the Communists, finally succeeding in getting the whole fleet out of Communist hands and back to the U. S. Only today, years later, is Communist China, again with British help, getting a modern air fleet.

This was what Chennault called his miracle No. 3.

Miracle No. 2 had been the Fourteenth Air Force. Miracle No. 1 was the AVG. Miracle No. 4 was in process. It was an international volunteer group, an IVG, to employ the superiority of air power in under-developed Asia to halt the Communists in Laos and Vietnam, using Czech, Polish and West German pilots, and any fighting pilot who hated Communists. If the General had lived and been successful, miracle No. 4 might have changed the situation in Asia, especially Laos and Vietnam today. But the General died from cancer. The Western world was too tired of imagination to let anyone else carry on miracle No. 4. It was not only tired of imagination, it was so rich it was tired of hard decisions. Like England and France in 1939, it preferred using money to buy time without trying to think through to the ultimate hard decisions it was buying time for.

Chapter 28

Death is a foe no mortal man—not even a Claire Chennault—can defeat. Long after the fall of China, long after CAT was a success, death finally came to my husband—but only after he had fought his usual courageous fight against his last enemy, cancer. The date was July 27, 1958, in a New Orleans hospital.

The struggle he made against the inevitable was an heroic one, made possible by the rugged constitution he had developed in his youth and preserved as a man, but more importantly, because of his flaming spirit. Claire Chennault fought death but never feared it, and faced it bravely, to the final moment.

The General lies at rest atop a grassy knoll overlooking Arlington, Robert E. Lee's home, and the Tomb of the Unknown Soldier. On the day of his funeral 5,000 of the world's great and small came to Arlington National Cemetery to pay final homage. Few men in one short lifetime had made so many enemies, so many more friends, accomplished so much with so little, been misunderstood so badly, and understood and loved so well. They had come to honor not only a Lieutenant General of the United States Air Force, but one of the most rugged American individuals, one of the most inspired and one of the best known—a man whose face, name, and famous deeds had caught the imagination of the entire world: the greatest Flying Tiger of them all, Chennault of China.

The Old Hero

A Tribute by
JOSEPH ALSOP, JR.

THE OLD HERO—by Joseph Alsop, Jr.

This story by Mr. Alsop appeared in his syndicated newspaper column "Matter of Fact" in 1958, a few days before the death of Claire L. Chennault. It is reprinted here with the permission of Mr. Alsop and the N.Y. Herald Tribune, *Inc.*

In these times when greater and greater dangers are monthly born of feebleness and folly, it is very good to think about the old hero, even on his deathbed. The Congress has just thought about him, graciously but belatedly promoting him to the rank of Lieutenant General in the U. S. Air Force.

But even the Congress cannot really have known much about the old hero. Almost no one knows, for instance, that he was one of the originators of the modern theory of airborne operations. The U. S. Army laughed at his theory, for cavalry was still more popular than airplanes in the mid-1920s. The Red Army offered him a rich contract to test his theory in the Soviet Union; but he refused it and that episode receded.

Almost no one knows, either, that he was almost certainly the leading American air ace of the Second World War—and this is hardly surprising, because the old hero rolled up his score of forty-odd Japanese airplanes shot down before we ever got into the war. That happened after they threw him out of the Air Force in the mid-1930s, merely because he was much, much too tactlessly right about the need for a balanced Air Force and a lot of other things. All the same, the Army doctors who certified that he was no longer fit for active service had quite good arguments on their side.

In fact the old hero was already deaf as a post and over 40 years old, when he turned up at Nanking just before the big Japanese attack on China. Possibly the Generalissimo and Madame Chiang Kai-shek did not know enough about modern medicine. At any rate, they found him fit enough to improvise the brilliant air defense of Nanking which utterly destroyed the first squadrons the Japanese sent in. And when the Chinese had no more planes of their own left, Madame Chiang, whom he loved, let the old hero go after the Japs himself, in his specially adapted Curtiss Hawk, on a straight piece-work basis.

That nest egg he made by shooting down Japanese bombers at $1000 per bomber was the "foreign money" the Army General Staff used to drop unpleasant hints about, when the old hero came to Washington to organize the American volunteer group—the "Flying Tigers" they called the group later, but I never liked the silly name. Out of little more than string and chewing gum, the old hero had devised the Chinese air warning net, that sustained

China's resistance through the worst years. Out of little more than string and chewing gum and some fine American pilots, he also devised the A. V. G.

One can see him now, sweating it out in the awful heat on that awful air field in Toungoo, Burma, in the pre-Pearl Harbor summer. Franklin Roosevelt had boldly given him 100 P-40s that even the beleaguered British did not want, and he had ground crews of 100 U. S. pilots of every imaginable sort. (Seven were actually Navy flying boat pilots, who first tried to land their P-40s about 15 feet above a steaming runway, with unfortunate consequences.) But he did not have any staff worth mentioning, or any spare parts at all, or even, for a while, any ammunition for his P-40's machine-guns.

Nobody but Diana Cooper and old Air Marshal Brooke-Popham, whom they later unjustly blamed for Singapore, really thought for a moment that the old hero could succeed in Burma. But there at Toungoo, he invented the radically new P-40 tactics that successfully defeated the Japanese Zeros. (They later decorated someone else for the invention.) Within a fortnight after he took the A. V. G. into China, no more Japanese bombs dropped. It was as simple as that, though he and the A. V. G. faced miracle odds of about five to one.

Again, one can see him now, as he was in those tangled, ugly war years at Kunming. By then you would have called him an old man—the skin of the deep-lined face was like the surface of long-aged oak—but the tremendous, telling jut of the jaw was still there all the same. He needed what that jutting jaw implied for his bitter wartime battles with the Air Staff, and that brave Gen. Joe Stilwell, and with a lot of other people.

The battles saved his Fourteenth Air Force, which in turn saved China from coming to pieces altogether in mid-war under the impact of the last Japanese offensive. (Very few people know it, but Stilwell's curious military plans never provided Chiang Kai-shek's worn-out infantry with a single machinegun bullet to use against the Japanese on any Chinese battlefield.) All the same, the old hero lost his last battle, to save Free China from the Communists.

Maybe he would have convinced more people more easily, maybe he would have to fight fewer battles, if he had fewer faults and weaknesses. He was almost wholly self-educated for one thing; and when he did his own logical calculation on the back of a dirty envelope, the results did not impress conventional-minded officers with staff training. For another, he had the touchy vanity that self-educated men with very great capacities always develop, if they are patronized and slighted as the old hero had been in his years in the peacetime U.S. Army.

There were some other warts to provide contrast in the portrait; but I have called him the old hero because he always remained a hero to me, although I studied the warts at closest range. His name is Claire Lee Chennault. We shall be poorer without him.

Men of Achievement

GENERAL GABRIEL P. DISOSWAY
Commander in Chief,
  United States Air Forces in Europe
and
Commander, 4th Allied Tactical Air Force

LIEUTENANT GENERAL BRUCE K. HOLLOWAY
Deputy Commander in Chief,
  US Strike Command

MAJOR GENERAL T. ALAN BENNETT
Director of Maintenance Engineering
  Hq Air Force Logistics Command

MAJOR GENERAL ROBERT A. BREITWEISER
Commander, USAF Southern Command
  (Old Caribbean Air Command)

MAJOR GENERAL WILLIAM P. FISHER
Deputy Commandant, Industrial College
  of the Armed Forces

MAJOR GENERAL JOHN K. HESTER
Assistant Vice Chief of Staff, USAF

Army

MAJOR GENERAL AUSTIN W. BETTS
  on duty with Atomic Energy Commission

RESERVE OF AIR FORCE OFFICERS (not on EAD)

MAJOR GENERAL JOHN R. ALISON
Mobilization Assistant to Commander,
  15th Air Force

MAJOR GENERAL CHARLES H. DU BOIS
Chief of Staff, Missouri ANG

BRIG. GENERAL CHARLES R. FOX
Former Adjutant General, West Virginia NG

Retired

MAJOR GENERAL ALBERT F. HOGENBERGER
MAJOR GENERAL REUBEN C. HOOD, Jr.
BRIG. GENERAL EUGENE H. BEEBE
BRIG. GENERAL MERIAN C. COOPER
BRIG. GENERAL JAMES L. JACKSON
BRIG. GENERAL BERTRAND E. JOHNSON
BRIG. GENERAL JOHN C. KENNEDY
BRIG. GENERAL RUSSELL E. RANDALL
BRIG. GENERAL ROBERT L. SCOTT
BRIG. GENERAL CLARENCE P. TALBOT
BRIG. GENERAL ROBERT W. C. WIMSATT
COLONEL FRED C. MILNER

Deceased

BRIG. GENERAL EDGAR E. GLENN
BRIG. GENERAL CLINTON D. VINCENT

Resigned Commission

BRIG. GENERAL SIDNEY D. GRUBBS

Civilians

MAX ABRAMOVITZ, Harrison & Abramovitz, New York
HENRY A. BYROADE, U. S. Ambassador
JACK MILLER, U. S. Senator, Ohio
GERHARD NEWMAN, Vice-President, General Electric

Index

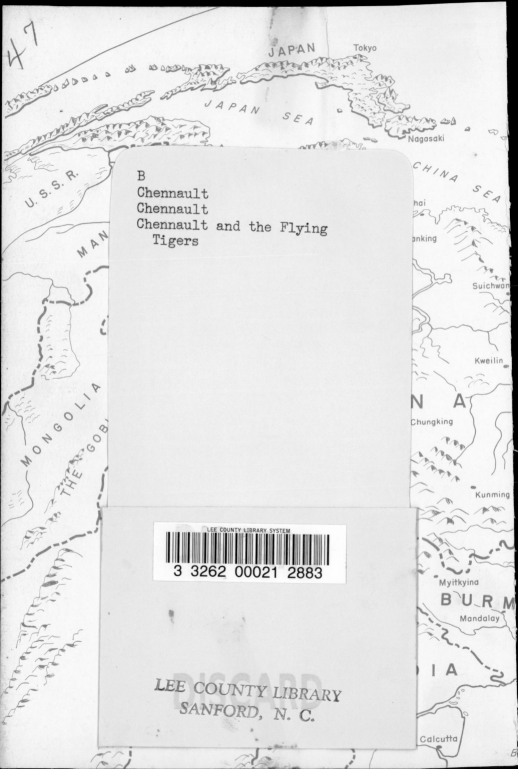

JAPAN Tokyo

JAPAN SEA

Nagasaki

U.S.S.R.

CHINA SEA

MAN

B
Chennault
Chennault
Chennault and the Flying
Tigers

hai

nking

Suichwan

Kweilin

N A

Chungking

MONGOLIA

THE GOB

Kunming

Myitkyina

B U R M

Mandalay

I A

Calcutta